PROJECT MANAGEMENT

Starter Guide for Beginners

3 BOOKS IN 1

By

Bryan Oliver

© **2019 by Bryan Oliver. All Rights Reserved.**

Thank you for taking the time to read this bundle. This starter guide has three of my best selling titles with some added bonus material at the end. This bundle is for those looking to kickstart their project management careers or for those looking refresh some critical skills.

The three books included cover **Project Manament for Beginners, Project Management – Emotional Intelligence**, and my book on **Habits**. This killer combination will give you the critical tools to make you stand out among your peers.

I hope you enjoy this bundle.

All the best,

Bryan

Table of Contents

Project Management: Secrets Successful Project Managers Know and What You Can Learn From Them

Introduction 9
   Who is this Book for? 9
   What You Will Learn 10

What is a Project Manager and Why Companies Need You 12
   What is a Project? 13

Key Skills of a Project Manager 14

Getting the Job 33
   Interviewing Skills 33
   Tip #1 33
   Tip #2 34
   Tip # 3 35

Doing the Job – Phases of a Project 37

Beyond Project Management 45

Glossary of terms 47

Project Management: Emotional Intelligence

Introduction 56

What is Project Management EQ, and why is it important?... 58

It's All About You 61

It's All About Them 70

Self-Management.. 83

Relationship Management 107

Conclusion... 125

Resources 127

HABITS: *CREATE WHAT YOU NEED TO SUCCEED IN LIFE*

Habit # 1: Surround yourself with healthy, like-minded people 133

Habit #2: Provide value 138

Habit #3: Do more than what's expected. 144

Habit #4: Understand personality styles. 149

Habit #5: Do what you know, not what you feel 157

Habit #6: Practice servant leadership 163

Habit #7: Be a professional learner 169

Habit #8: Exercise 173

Habit #9: Protect your thoughts 177

Habit #10: Take action 182

Putting It All Together 186

Conclusion 193

About the Author 204

Project Management:
Secrets Successful Project Managers Know and What You Can Learn From Them

A Beginner's Guide to Project Management With Tips On Learning The Essential Soft Skills To Manage A Project Like A Pro

By

Bryan Oliver

Introduction

Who is this Book for?

This book is meant for those who have little to no experience in project management and is by no means a replacement for the extensive study and art of project management. Yes, I said art. This book will address more of the art involved in project management; you will learn some high-level project management methodology. At the back of the book, I have included a glossary, so you have a reference of some of the most common used terms in project management, and this book will cover the high-level overview of the phases of a project. At the end of the book, I have also provided a few resources for you to further your education in project management.

What You Will Learn

This book is not a quick fix and does not replace the years of experience and study of the most seasoned and successful project managers. However, there are some key skills and tips you need to learn when it comes to succeeding in a project management interview and dealing with your teams and stakeholders. If applied early and often, these skills can and will set you apart from the majority of project managers out there. Why? I'm so glad you asked. The reason is most likely focus. The field of project management is not easy and takes many years to become proficient. Most of the average project managers I've worked with over the years focus on the tactical and technical approaches to project management. The elite-level project managers are experts at these approaches, but they take it a step further. They take the time to learn and implement these key skills, where the average project manager will not take the time to educate themselves.

I've been managing projects and project managers for the better part of 20 years now, and I have to say my career has been extremely rewarding. If you are looking to get into project management or just starting out, you've come to the right place. You are embarking on an amazing journey which has some fantastic rewards. But, make no mistake, you will need to work hard, and if you want to be one of the best, you will need to do more than just learn to manage a project. I'm excited to share with you what I've learned from my own personal experiences and through the experiences of the many phenomenal project managers I've had the privilege of working with and serving over the years.

What is a Project Manager and Why Companies Need You

According to Wikipedia, "a project manager is a professional in the field of project management. Project managers can have the responsibility of the planning, execution, and closing of any project, typically relating to the construction industry, architecture, aerospace, and defense, computer networking, telecommunications or software development". For executives of a company, the benefits of having a project manager are many. However, the true value of a project manager comes in the form of cost savings, reduced risk, and improved success rates on projects.

What is a Project?

There are various interpretations and definitions of what a project is. This book defines a project with the following criteria:

- A project is temporary, meaning it has a predetermined beginning and end date.
- A project has a unique set of tasks, meaning what is performed during a project will not necessarily be done on an ongoing basis as part of a company's daily operations.
- Has a defined scope and specific set of resources to be used

Key Skills of a Project Manager

Over the years, I have worked with and interviewed hundreds of project managers. The best ones I've worked with are experts in the follow areas.

Communication and building rapport

In every interview I conduct, I ask the following question, "What do you believe are the top 3 skills a project manager should have?" Of all the many different answers I get, the one I am always looking for communication. I am ok if they don't say this first, but they must speak about it, or the rest of the interview typically goes south. Being able to effectively communicate with your project teams and stakeholders is critical for the success of the project.

As a project manager, you must be able to provide accurate and thorough updates to those that need to have information in order to make appropriate decisions. Unfortunately, sometimes you'll need to be the bearer of bad news. Your job as the project manager is to ensure any news or status is communicated, and if something is wrong, you need to be able to communicate the mitigation plan. You can make the communication process easier by building a connection with your team and project sponsors.

One particular project manager I know takes the time to get to know each individual on her team before the project kicks off. If she is in the same office, she sets up an in person meeting to further build a connection. By doing this, she learns what is important to them and where their roadblocks and challenges exist. You'd be surprised how often project managers sit behind their computers and only communicate with their team via email, instant message, and the occasional conference call, rarely taking the time to build a relationship with team members or those paying for the project.

💡 ***Pro Tip:*** When getting to know your team members, ask them about previous projects and where the major "gotchas" were. By doing this, you are showing them that you respect and value their experience, and you are there to help prevent the pain points they previously experienced. People are more than willing to work with you at crunch time or go above and beyond when you need them to if they LIKE, TRUST, and RESPECT you.

Be Organized with Attention to Detail

Projects are comprised of many moving parts. In order to be effective, you'll need to be well organized and pay close attention to detail. Although having knowledge and experience may be a job requirement, it doesn't mean you will need to be an expert at specific project management software. If you are just beginning your project management job, the chances are you will not be required to have thorough knowledge of software like Microsoft Project. However, you will be expected to keep track of all pieces of the project and be able to provide status in any given area and at any given time. For this, you need to make sure you are well organized and are paying close attention to the details of project. Depending on the company, you will need to take the time to learn the budget, changes, and any project management systems that are in place. Some use out-of-box software, like MS Project, and others have in-house systems. Your role and responsibility as a project manager is to be familiar with these systems and effectively utilize them in the manner your client requires.

Leadership

Leadership is a characteristic I often see missing in many project managers. There is a big difference between being part of a project and leading a project. To be effective and successful, project managers need to develop strong leadership skills.

What is a leader?

A leader does the following:

1) Inspires a vision for what the future will look like
2) Motivates the team to want to be part of that vision
3) Oversees the delivery and success of that vision
4) Coaches, mentors, and builds up the team to increase the effectiveness of executing the vision

Pro Tip: Understand that your team wants the project to succeed, and they are looking to you to guide them to victory. Take every opportunity to motivate, encourage, and make a connection with your team. If they know you have their back, they will have yours.

Intuition

Intuition is a skill that is innate in everyone, and to a certain degree, it cannot be coached. When it comes to project management, intuition is developed over time and through experience. Do you ever wonder how some people can anticipate something going wrong at work and prevent it from going too far? This is their intuition at play. If you are new in your career, you can practice this by trying to anticipate the next move in small areas of your project. Some of the best lessons you will learn to build your intuition will come from making mistakes. Don't let these mistakes discourage you. It's part of the process, and you need to learn from it and adjust accordingly. In order to be at the top of your game, you need to work on developing this skill.

💡 ***Pro Tip:*** Find senior project managers that are willing to mentor you. Ask them a lot of questions. You will begin to see a pattern in the way some of the best pick up on issues that may arise. Most people are willing to share their experiences, so utilize these great resources.

People Skills

This section is taken from the personality styles section of my book *Habits: Create What You Need To Succeed In Life*. This skill and habit will not only set you apart from other project managers, but it will serve as a strong foundation for your future career success. I cannot emphasize enough how much positive impact this particular skill has had on my career.

Your personality related to how you tend to think, feel, and behave—is shaped by your genetic makeup as well as your life experiences. Our personalities determine the way we interact with people in our life. Understanding the power of our personality will help prepare us to attain success.

Part of being a successful and competent individual in the workplace is to know your strengths, weaknesses, communication skills, and learning styles. There are many excellent personality assessments that can assist you with discovering more about yourself. As you learn more about your own personality type, it is imperative that you learn more about the personality types of others.

There are four basic personality types. Depending on the personality test you take, the names may be different. The four main personality types are:

1. Type A

2. Analytical

3. Feeler

4. Expressive

People who are Type A tend to focus on fact rather than emotion. They are driven to see measurable results, and their intensity may make them quick to offend people, even though that may not be their intention. Type A personalities like to act quickly and are enthusiastic about tackling projects and seeing results. If you want something done, call a person with a Type A personality.

Analytical personalities like to amass details and comb through them first rather than acting hastily. They value accuracy in their work and expect the same precision and excellence from others. They relate to Ben Franklin's motto, "Everything has a place and everything in its place."

People with Feeler personalities are people-centric and value meaningful relationships.

This personality style makes for great team players, as people with this personality type are patient and want to interact with their coworkers on a personal level. They are revealing when it comes to the events of their life, hope to know others, and are sensitive to the feelings of others. If you need someone to talk to, go find someone with the Feeler personality. They can talk through issues with you and are willing to help if they can.

Those with Expressive personalities are creative and astute in the art of persuasion. Because they are enthusiastic and friendly, expressive personality, people value communicating with others and thrive when the lines of communication are open. Expressive personalities long for recognition and often need support to reign in their many ideas in order to achieve specific goals.

It is important to remember that no one person fits perfectly into one category. Each individual is likely to express characteristics that are indicative to all four types, with a greater emphasis on one or two. These categories are not meant to put people into behavioral boxes. Instead, they are meant to help us better understand each other's tendencies. These characteristics can help us understand the deeper motivations of each member on your team, including the most important person, yourself.

To understand your own personality and where you tend to lean, consider taking an in-depth personality test like Myers-Briggs or Strengthsfinder 2.0. Learning your personality type will be an ongoing process and study for the remainder of your career. Once you've gained a basic framework of your personality, the next step is to learn about the other three styles and how they work together. As a leader of your projects, you will need to understand your team's personality style and tendencies in order to get the most value for the project.

💡 ***Pro Tip:*** Become an expert on your personality style and start to identify others with a similar style. After that, you can do a deep dive into the other personalities and learn the nuances and gifts each person brings to the team.

Emotional Intelligence

IQ is often talked about relative to how smart, and successful someone is. Less talked about, but just as to the success in project management is emotional intelligence (EQ). Your EQ is measured by how well you are aware of and in control of your emotions. Having a high EQ allows you to adapt quickly and empathize with your project team and stakeholders. High EQ also allows you to overcome obstacles which are sure to arise in your project and deal with conflict management. Let's take a look at these situations in a little more detail.

Projects change and evolve daily, and sometimes hourly. Your success will depend on your ability to adapt to these constant changes. Remember that you will be faced with unforeseeable obstacles, and there will be people on your team with their own agendas, as well. It is important that you weed out any conflicts and align with those who share your vision and the end goal of the project. All this will be going on while you are motivating and guiding your team to the finish line. To become the best project manager, you must become an expert in managing all these areas. In order to do that, you must look for ways to increase your emotional intelligence. I will provide a couple of good book references for you at the end of this book should you decide to go into a deeper study on emotional intelligence.

Pro Tip: Make it a practice to not immediately respond or participate in a heated email or instant message debate. If you disagree with something you are reading, wait 24 hours, formulate your answer in an unemotional state, then respond. Emotionally responding to any form of communication, especially email, can severely limit your career potential – yes, read this as 'get your fired.'

Customer Service

This is probably one of the key areas I see many project managers fall short on. Many of us are very process driven and have an incredible ability to drive a project through the project phases to closure on time and on budget. While this is fantastic, some forget whom they are working for and the reason they are employed. "But who is the customer?" you might be asking yourself. Always remember that your stakeholder is your customer. While it is true that your stakeholder is your end customer, keep in mind that there are many other people you will be dealing with.

For example, I contend that your team is also your customer and that you are there to serve them. The thing you need to remember is that without your team, your project will not get done. I've seen many project managers take the approach of pounding the table and pushing for performance with no regard for those on the team. Most of these folks don't last very long in their roles. On the flip side, I've seen some project managers provide some amazing customer service, and they have a team that will go the distance for them. As a by-product of this behavior, their projects are successfully completed, and the stakeholders come back with more work. Can you see the difference here? You can literally create longevity in your career by providing exceptional customer service.

Pro Tip: View each of your team members as your customer. Look for ways you can exceed their expectations and provide better service to them.

Influence

As a project manager, you will typically not have anyone that directly reports to you. Rather, you will be managing resources that are part of the organization. These resources have their own managers and are working on other projects, in addition to yours. In other words, you will need to influence without authority.

In order to effectively complete your project, you will need to influence the resources on your team to do what is needed for the project. Sometimes, this will come at a time when they have competing priorities. We previously spoke about Emotional Intelligence, and this is where this skill comes into play. You must be fully aware of the situation your resources are in, have empathy, and look for ways to help them succeed, not only in your project but in their other projects as well. By showing them you understand their situation and you are empathetic toward them, you stand a good chance at gaining their loyalty.

💡 ***Pro Tip:*** Get to know your teams outside of the work they do. What are their hobbies? Do they have children? You can better influence someone when you know and understand their personal wants, needs, and desires.

Stakeholder Management

A stakeholder is someone that has a vested interest in the project you are leading. Managing your stakeholders is as much of an art as it is a skill. There will be some stakeholders that will want early and often communication, while others just want high-level updates once or every other week. It is up to you to ask them how often they'd like communication and to what level. While this sounds like a fairly simple task, you'd be surprised how many project managers fail in this area. My belief is they fail because they assume all stakeholders are alike and receive information in the same way. Some will want very detailed updates, while others just want to know if the project is on track and if there are any issues or risks. Assuming all stakeholders want the same things may cause you to be viewed as ineffective in the eyes of some. Unfortunately, you will not please everyone, but you do need to understand those that need pleasing and communicate accordingly.

💡 ***Pro Tip:*** Identify early which stakeholders will be your allies and which will be your opponents. In larger projects, you will find some stakeholders who have their own agendas, and your project is not one of their priorities. As a matter of fact, you may have a stakeholder who wants your project to fail, so they can highlight and provide credence to something on their agenda.

Conflict Management

If you are running a project, you will experience conflict. It may be directed at you, or you may have conflict within the team. Either way, developing the skills to effectively manage conflict will move your project along and could potentially save it from a disastrous failure. Understanding the personality styles and building those relationships early on will help you when conflict arises.

💡 ***Pro Tip:*** When conflict arises, don't try to exert your authority in a public setting. This will only serve to put the person in conflict on the defensive and make them want to prove their point further. Instead, set up some time with the person or persons, in private, and discuss the issue at hand. It may take a little extra time, but you will find it will save you significant time and aggravation later.

Getting the Job

Interviewing Skills

I am not going to bore you with interviewing tips you can glean from the thousands of websites out there. What I will provide are three things I look for when I'm interviewing someone and what I have found to be consistent with those that perform the best after they are hired. I have worked with and interviewed hundreds of project managers over the last 15 years. The ones that have left the strongest impressions mastered the following three tips.

Tip #1 Tell the Story before You're Asked

When I'm interviewing a potential candidate, I have a few expectations, which I don't share upfront. One of those expectations is that the candidate will answer some of my questions before I ever ask them, and the more senior the project manager, the more detail I expect them to provide.

Here's an example. A common question in an interview goes something like, "Tell me about your experience." Before you interview, do your homework on the types of questions that are typically asked of a project manager and address those questions in your story about your experience. The more experience you have, the more detailed your explanations will be. If you have little to no experience, draw information from your part-time jobs, school projects, or volunteering to shape your story and answer questions you might be asked. It's rare, but I've had interviews where I asked the candidate just one question, and they answered the rest of my questions in the story. Needless to say, I recommended the person for hire immediately.

Tip #2 Make Your Weaknesses Your Strengths

A common question that is asked in an interview, especially when you have little to no experience, is, "Tell me about your strengths and weaknesses." You can effectively answer this question by discussing your weaknesses and showing the interviewer how you've turned that weakness into a strength. Everyone has weaknesses, so you might as well figure out what yours are and learn to make them your strengths. On top of this, explain how you have applied this strength, so they see you in action.

Tip # 3 Be Interested in Them

We all listen to the same radio station WIIFM – What's in it for me. In an interview, it's your job to relate to the interviewer and not the other way around. Consider the interviewer as the gatekeeper to the company you are trying to join. They have their own interests and what they care about, so make sure you understand what they are.

You can do this by taking an honest and sincere interest in them and their company. A great way to kill your interview is if you are asked, "Tell me what you know about our company," and you either give some generic answer or speak out some quotes from their website. Here's a secret for you. The last ten people they interviewed said the same thing. Really learn about the company and learn about the interviewer. Understand the company's position in the market place, who their competitors are, and what their differentiator is. If you can't find that information on the internet, those are good questions for you to ask when you are given the opportunity.

Also, you will often be given the name(s) of the people that will be interviewing you. You can head over to LinkedIn and learn about them. Not that you want to stalk them, but you can learn more about them on Facebook and other social media sites. Don't think for a minute they are not checking out your social media footprint. If the company is truly a good fit for you, there will be common interests and interesting facts you will want to know about. After all, you will be spending 40 plus hours a week with these people, so you want to make sure you like them and vice versa.

Doing the Job – Phases of a Project

The following is an overview of the phases of a project. It is by no means meant to be an all-inclusive list. If you are just starting out as a project manager or looking to get into project management, this chapter will provide some key items you will need to know in order to successfully manage a project. If you are looking to further study the field of project management, the Project Management Institute is a great place to start. There are also hundreds of websites for you to gain some insight. I have put some resources at the end of this book to get you started. Above all else, there is no substitute for experience to really learn how these phases work on a daily basis.

Initiation

Before a project even begins, there is certain alignment that needs to occur between the stakeholders, those who are paying for the project. The first thing that happens is that an idea is presented. The idea will present the goals and scope of the project, the benefits to the organization, possible high-level cost estimates, and potential risks for doing or not doing the project. Once the idea is presented, feasibility needs to be determined. Depending on the size of the project, feasibility may have already been done before the idea is presented, to strengthen the case of the proposal. From here, the project will need stakeholder commitment. Once the project is committed to, the next component is ready to begin, and that is the drafting and approval of the project charter. The project's charter will outline the scope of the project as well as provide assumptions and high-level requirements. Also included in the project charter is a high level schedule overview, which is an outline of the resources needed, project milestones, and a communication plan that will be used for the duration of the project. From here, you are ready to begin planning.

Planning

During planning, you will begin the project by inviting all the necessary resources you have found. Some organizations have resource assignment mechanisms that can help you determine who these individuals are. If you don't have such a mechanism and are part of a smaller organization, you will need to speak to your department heads to determine if their involvement may be needed.

Execution, Control, and Monitoring

Once you have a plan for the project, it's time to begin execution. During the execution, you will be working on the Control and Monitoring phase at that same time. The first thing you will need to do is have a working session with your team and run through the schedule. Depending on the size of your team, you can do this as one large group or meet with each team member individually. I've done it both ways, and the larger group has worked better for smaller projects.

As the work begins, you need to start a cadence of weekly team meetings and status reports, so the stakeholders' have a good idea of where the project stands. In the status report, you'll need to include an overview of the project description, completed and upcoming milestones, any significant accomplishments, along with risks and issues. What you must understand when it comes to the status report is that your stakeholder, typically executives, will glance at your report for less than a minute. In a larger organization, the stakeholders are responsible for quite a number of projects and usually have very little time to go into the details. So, your job is to highlight the major components of the project in as short a space as possible. This includes providing enough detail so they understand any risks or issues and if they need to take any action.

Throughout the execution of the project, you need to monitor and control how the project is doing. Your job as a project manager, as I mentioned earlier, is to anticipate issues that may arise, act on them, and control the situation. This is done through active engagement with your project team. Often, this will occur on a weekly basis, but many times, depending on where you are in the project, you may need to speak to them daily and possibly even hourly. At the most basic level, however, you will need consistent updates from your team so you know where the project stands so you can assist your team to get them where they need to be. This also becomes critical when the need arises to escalate to your leadership.

Escalation Dos and Don'ts

Escalations are often viewed as a bad thing when, in reality, there are times when you need the leader's help to move your project along. An escalation can be an effective tool to bring awareness and help your project succeed. Here are some dos and don'ts when it comes to escalation.

Do:

- Escalate early.
- Be clear and concise in your messages.
- Give a heads up to those you are escalating on.
- Provide a solution to the problem with a timeline to resolve issues.
- State the facts.
- Give your resource a deadline and give them the opportunity to succeed. They need to know ahead of time that an escalation is forthcoming if the deadline is not met.

Don't

- Be accusatory
- Surprise your leadership with an escalation (leadership does not like surprises)
- Give a long winded explanation, even though you believe one is needed
- Send out an escalation before telling the resource being escalated on.

💡 ***Pro Tip:*** Your project will typically not be the only thing your resources are responsible for. You will find they will react most to the "squeaky wheel." This is where your people skills will come into play so you can get them to focus them on the objectives to get your project done while being mindful of their other duties and responsibilities.

Closure

This is the part of the project where you formally close the project. By this time, the work is complete and has moved into an operational state. In this phase, you will release your resources and tie up any loose ends related to the project. This is also a good time to recognize your team members and highlight anyone who did outstanding work for you during the project.

Beyond Project Management

In this book, you've learned what a project manager and the key skills needed to set you apart from others in your field. You also received some interview tips as well as some Pro Tips to give you an edge in your career. Whether you decide to make a career of project management or have a desire to move into people management, the skills and techniques you have learned in this book will set you apart from others, no matter which path you choose. Take the time to continue to learn new skills and create winning habits that will propel your career to new heights. To learn more on creating winning habits, you can just scroll down to the book included in this bundle. If you are looking to gain more comprehensive project management knowledge, I recommend you take an in person or online course on the subject. Also, you can purchase the Project Management Institute's book called the *Project Management*

Body of Knowledge (PMBOK). This book contains knowledge used in the Project Management Professional (PMP) and Certified Associate Project Management (CAPM) exams. For the requirements needed to take these exams, please visit the Project Management Institute.

Glossary of terms

(Reprinted courtesy of Wikipedia.org and released under CC-BY-SA)

The following is not a complete list but rather the most commonly used terms you will need to be familiar with as a project manager. For a full A-Z list, you can visit Wikipedia here.

Allocation is the assignment of available resources in an economic way.

Budget generally refers to a list of all planned expenses and revenues.

Change control is the procedures used to ensure that changes (normally, but not necessarily, to IT systems) are introduced in a controlled and coordinated manner. Change control is a major aspect of the broader discipline of change management.

Change management is a field of management focused on organizational changes. It aims to ensure that methods and procedures are used for efficient and prompt handling of all changes to controlled IT infrastructure in order to minimize the number and impact of any related incidents upon service.

Critical path is the sequence of project network activities, which add up to the longest overall duration, regardless if that longest duration has float or not. This determines the shortest time possible to complete the project.

Dependency in a project network is a link amongst a project's terminal elements.

Deliverable A contractually required work product, produced and delivered to a required state. A deliverable may be a document, hardware, software, or other tangible product.

Gantt chart is a type of bar chart that illustrates a project schedule. It illustrates the start and finish dates of the terminal elements and summary elements of a project. Terminal elements and summary elements comprise the work breakdown structure of the project.

Issue – An error that has occurred during the course of a project that may affect the budget or schedule. Issues are typically tracked in an issue log.

Kickoff meeting is the first meeting with the project team and the client of the project.

Level of Effort (LOE) is qualified as a support type activity which doesn't lend itself to measurement of a discrete accomplishment. Examples of such an activity may be project budget accounting, customer liaison, etc.

Project plan is a formal, approved document used to guide both *project execution* and *project control*. The primary uses of the project plan are to document planning assumptions and decisions, facilitate communication among *stakeholders*, and document approved scope, cost, and schedule *baselines*. A project plan may be summary or detailed

Project team is the management team leading the project and provide services to the project. Projects often bring together a variety number of problems. Stakeholders have important issues with others

Resources are what is required to carry out a project's tasks. They can be people, equipment, facilities, funding, or anything else capable of definition (usually other than labour) required for the completion of a project activity

Risk is the precise probability of specific eventualities.

Scope of a project in project management is the sum total of all of its products and their requirements or features

Tasks in project management are activity that needs to be accomplished within a defined period of time

Work Breakdown Structure (WBS) is a tool that defines a project and groups the project's discrete work elements in a way that helps organize and define the total work scope of the project. A Work breakdown structure element may be a product, data, a service, or any combination. WBS also provides the necessary framework for detailed cost estimating and control along with providing guidance for schedule development and control

Project Management: Emotional Intelligence

By

Bryan Oliver

Disclaimer: Although the author and publisher have made every effort to ensure that the information in this book was correct at press time, the author and publisher do not assume and hereby disclaim any liability to any party for any loss, damage, or disruption caused by errors or omissions, whether such errors or omissions result from negligence, accident, or any other cause.

Introduction

Over my career, I've had the opportunity to work with some incredible project managers. If I'm honest, there was a period of time where I thought project management was not my calling, especially when I compared myself these aforementioned project managers. The truth is, just about everything I do is a project and how I deal with people affects my productivity, happiness, income, stress, along with just about every aspect of my life. As I reflect, what made these successful project managers so effective was not only possessing the technical knowledge - they knew how to execute and deliver all phases related to the project lifecycle.

In addition to being skilled at delivery, a great project manager needs to have a high degree of Emotional Intelligence. For this book, we will refer to Emotional Intelligence, also known as Emotional Intelligence Quotient, by using the EQ designation. Those great project managers

I've worked with in the past, and work with today, have a high EQ.

Although this book is written for the *beginner/novice* project manager, the lessons taught will apply to all levels of project management, and quite frankly are universal for just about all your business endeavors. Even the most experienced project manager will be able to elevate their effectiveness by increasing their EQ. So, if you, too, are seeking the road for a more effective team experience and project success, then get ready for a journey to increase your EQ.

What is Project Management EQ, and why is it important?

Emotional Intelligence was popularized by Dan Goleman in 1996 and is often credited as the cornerstone of leadership within organizations. When looking at project management emotional intelligence, we must first define what emotional intelligence is. Emotional intelligence, for the purposes of this book, is being aware of your own emotions while also being aware of the emotions of others. In addition, it's your ability to influence the emotions of others while controlling your own emotions.

A project manager who is emotionally intelligent is able to perform at a higher level because she more acutely aware of her surroundings and of others in her circle of influence. In addition, she is able to build healthy and effective relationships, allowing her to be more effective as a project manager. The stronger her relationships are, the greater her chances are for being successful in the delivery of her projects.

Here's one for those of you that are focused on increasing your bottom line. According to talentsmart.com, the majority of top earners possess high EQ: "people with high EQ make $29K more, annually than their low EQ counterparts." Is it worth your time and investment to increase your EQ?

What Makes This Book Different?

Though EQ has many platforms to be learned, this book targets EQ as it relates to you as a project manager. You'll journey through true examples and scenarios of project management, where the successful use of EQ played an integral role in the overall success of the project manager.

The pmi.org's *A Guide to the Project Management Body of Knowledge (PMBOK® Guide)* outlines the "whats," "hows and "whys" of project management and even lists some effective tools and techniques for performing project tasks. But, and not to my surprise, it leaves the development of one's "soft skills," a.k.a. EQ, up to the individual project manager and team.

A project manager can have all the technical skills known to man, but if she is not able to balance the technical with the soft skills, she will not be living up to her highest potential and, at best, will be considered ~~be~~ average and easily overlooked. Without effective soft skills, especially the EQ component, her future success as an accomplished, recognized, and in-demand project manager will be limited.

It's All About You

A Project Manager's Self-Awareness

Putting yourself first isn't always easy, but it is fundamental when learning a new skill or thought process. Understanding how you react to others and the situations you are in is the first step to increasing your project management emotional intelligence.

Several years ago, I was working alongside project manager Matt, who was several years my senior when it came to project management experience. I looked up to him and, quite frankly, wanted to be just like him. That is, until this one project.

The project we worked on was a multi-year infrastructure project and required the replacement of hundreds of networking components. We had teams from all over the world and in almost every state in the United States. The effort was very large and complex.

As we started the project, Matt was in control. You could tell he was very experienced and knew how to run a project. His documentation was organized, he understood what to do in the beginning phases, and he effectively communicated the expectations of the project to our team during the project kickoff.

Several weeks into our efforts, the business decided on a change in direction. Due to a budget shortage, the project timeline had to be shortened in order for the project to have adequate funding. While this is not uncommon, it does add pressure ~~to~~ on the project manager, ~~but~~ as well as the entire Even the most seasoned of project managers can cope with the changing of a previously agreed upon budget and scope, but only for so long.

About two months after the initial discovery of budget constraints, you could tell the pressure was starting to mount on Matt. His frustration was palpable to the rest of our team. This was especially true in our meetings with both the core team as well as those with vendors and business stakeholders. He was easily agitated, highly frustrated, and, like an open wound, extremely vulnerable. Everyone noticed that he was starting to get flustered much quicker and easier now. Where he used to be calm as gentle tides rolling in, he was now emotionally volatile, crashing like storm waves. Symptoms of the changes within the project caused delays in the equipment delivery, and due to budget cuts, team members were given added work from other projects. This meant they did not have the same amount of time to devote to our project as they did when we started.

In retrospect, I now realize that I was witnessing Matt's particular level of emotional intelligence in action. His emotional intelligence "playbook" if you will. The more pressure Matt was under, the easier it became to read the stress in his face, hear it in his voice, and observe it in his interactions with others. Matt's low level of emotional intelligence did not equip him to be self-aware of his actions or to realize his deteriorating perception amongst the team and others.

So, as a project manager, what can you do to become more self-aware and therefore increase your emotional intelligence? Let's look at the following three ways you can increase your self-awareness.

1) Assess Yourself

You are your own greatest ally and asset, so make time for a self-assessment. Take time to familiarize yourself with your strengths and weaknesses. This is not meant as an exercise for you to judge yourself harshly, or pat yourself on the back. This exercise is simply for you to evaluate where you are. The answers you reveal are neither good nor bad; they just are so you can hold that mirror up to yourself and really be honest.

Next, in your self-assessment, you will want to understand your triggers. What are those things that cause you to get upset, lose control, or get sidetracked? Are you an emotional elevator? Admittedly, grasping a good understanding of my own triggers was a tenuous task and one that took a long time for me to understand. However, once I understood how these triggers were impacting my life, I decided to make some changes. I've listed a few of these personal learnings, so you have an idea of some of the things you can work on. This is not an exhaustive list, and some of these may not apply to you. I encourage you to evaluate your own situation and honestly assess what triggers you to act in a negative way. With that, here is what I did:

    a. I stopped watching the news. I realized that watching the news each day was allowing a lot of negativity into my life. The constant barrage of political garbage and the overall bad news was doing nothing to lift me up. On the contrary, I realized it was affecting my attitude and the conversations I would have with those around me. Aside from the occasional weather report or stock market check, I avoid the news channels like the plague.

b. I limited my time spent and involvement with social media. Excessive involvement with social media involvement wasted a lot of my time, and like the news, I was seeing and watching a lot of negative opinions flow through my feed each day. The negativity witnessed triggered an equally negative attitude, which ultimately bled into my overall effectiveness as a husband, father, and project manager.

c. I adjusted my reaction to others emotions. Instead, I chose to understand their point of view first and not immediately react to them emotionally. I first had to admit to myself that I was easily influenced by the emotions of others. Some people don't like that approach because it is not easy to do. Also, revealing a weakness, let alone working on it, is not something many are willing to do.

d. Probably the biggest lesson I learned was to understand that I am an introvert and knowing my emotional limits. As a project manager, you are constantly around people, and for an introvert, too much people interaction is mentally and emotionally exhausting. At first, I used "being an introvert" as an excuse to avoid the people interactions and relationship building that is so critical in successful project management Over time, I also learned that I could exercise my "people muscle," which enabled me to spend more time around others without getting as tired. But, learning what enabled me also helped me to recognize what triggered my limitations. At my core, I'm still an introvert, so you won't see me socializing for hours on end like my extroverted counterparts. However, I have learned to work through this important skill of interacting with others. Without this understanding, I would have never known or thought how I could have taken my greatest strengths as an introvert and expand them to be a better project manager and leader.

Making yourself aware of your triggers and shortcomings can assist you in making some minor adjustments when you deal with and react to your surroundings.

2) Ask Others To Assess You

After you've taken the time to evaluate yourself, ask others around you to assess your strengths and weaknesses. This exercise can be done on a personal and professional level. However, since we are discussing project management, find those that you have worked with on recent projects. Some may feel that you are looking for some kudos or ego stroke, but make sure to let them know you are trying to get an honest assessment of your strengths and weaknesses.

Assure them that this effort is so you can improve as a project manager and professional.

3) Complete A Formal Assessment

There are several assessments you can take online to assess your emotional intelligence. Some are free, and some are paid. Pick one that works the best for you so you can get a good idea of where you sit on an EQ level. You'll find some resources for you in the resource section of the book.

It's All About Them

A Project Manager's Social Awareness

Once you begin to understand yourself, your emotions, what makes you tick, and your triggers, then you can start to understand others around you.

Let's go back and analyze Matt's social awareness for a moment. As mentioned, he began to show frustration in his interactions with all of us. What he didn't realize was how his reactions were affecting the team and his effectiveness with the team. With Matt's lack of social awareness, he missed some critical clues that would have brought the team together and made the project run much smoother. What Matt was missing, in the area of social awareness, is some of what we are about to cover.

Are you a reader?

Not to be mistaken with reading scholastically, but are you a reader of people? High social awareness comes with the ability to read people. Can you read their faces, their body language, or understand the differences in tone when they are speaking? A project manager's ability to read people and the situation is a key differentiator between the average and great project managers. Let's look a little deeper at how you can develop the skills necessary to read people and situations. These skills ~~alone~~ will make you stand out as a project manager and a leader.

Reading People

There are three areas to focus on when it comes to reading people. One is reading their faces or their micro-expressions, second is reading their body language, and third is listening closely to their voice or their tone. Understanding how to read people can save you a lot of time and heartache personally and professionally. Let's first take a look at the micro-expressions.

Micro Expressions

Have you ever been in a conversation with someone and noticed that they made a face when you said something. Most of us dismiss these facial expressions and continue with our conversation. But, what if you were to start learning what these micro expressions are, what they mean, and how to react to them? Maybe you'll become known as the face whisperer. Ok, maybe not. But, you will be able to pick up on subtleties that most never will. Most of this simply has to do with understanding what these expressions mean and then simply observing. According to Dr. Paul Ekman, a former psychology professor at the University of California at San Francisco and researcher on nonverbal behavior, as it relates to facial expressions and gestures, "Whether we live in China, Cuba, or Canada, all of us express the same seven universal emotions of anger, fear, sadness, disgust, surprise, contempt, and happiness." Dr. Ekman was also the advisor to the popular television show, *Lie To Me*.

Let's look at a couple of these expressions and discuss how you can apply them to your daily life as a project manager.

Surprise and Anger

These two emotions often go hand in hand because one either triggers or follows the other. For instance, if you are sharing a delay in a project, your stakeholder may be surprised, and, since you are communicating a delay, this may be followed by anger. Later we'll discuss why you never want to surprise a stakeholder. For now, become aware of the micro expressions after you've delivered your message to your stakeholder. You will want to make sure the words and actions that the stakeholder is communicating are congruent with the micro expressions they are displaying. The reason for this is some may show that everything is ok, but then go straight to your boss or theirs and report their discontent. It's not that you will be able to stop them, but if you can understand the micro expression, it gives you an opportunity to engage further conversation with them to bring their apprehension down and show how you have a solution or, at a minimum, show you are in control of your project. At the same time, you'll want to anticipate what their next move will be based on their expression. Also, if no further words are spoken, you can at least give your superiors the heads up on what happened and the fact that the person you delivered the message to was not happy. Again, no surprises for your boss are a good idea as well.

Contempt

Why would it be a good idea to understand the contempt micro expression? Contempt is the opposite of empathy. It leans more toward arrogance and not caring what someone is going through and only concerned with oneself. So, if you delivered the same news to your boss as above and you show a micro expression of contempt, your boss would think you really don't care that there is a delay in delivery. Understanding this would allow you to direct further discussion to solutions and options that would benefit your boss and her concerns.

One thing to understand, which will come in a future book and is a large component of project management, is the cultural aspects of these micro-expressions. Different cultures have different ways of expressing the aforementioned expressions. Reading these expressions the wrong way can have outcomes in the exact opposite way that you intended.

We've only scratched the surface, and this is by no means an exhausted list of micro-expressions, but if you take the time to study this type of facial recognition, you can learn to communicate and anticipate more effectively.

Body Language

Body language, while not always so subtle as the micro expressions you will see on someone's face, can give you an edge when speaking to someone and help with your relatability to that person. Let's take a look at what Matt taught me about body language.

After several months on the project, you could see Matt's body language change. He was more slumped over, shoulders rolled forward, and his head was more down than it was up. I could tell something was wrong, but I had not yet developed the skills to know what I was observing. However, luckily for Matt, someone in the room did. They must have spoken to him because a week later, in our next meeting, he was sitting up straight, his voice was more forceful, and you could tell he had command of the room. I was very curious about what had changed, so I asked him, and this is what he told me.

Matt told me that someone had pointed out how his body language was being perceived and how that contributed to how he was acting. He went on to tell me that he no idea he was doing this but was feeling more and more pressure as the project went on. I was still curious, so I asked him to tell me more about what he learned.

Confidence

One of the first things a project manager must convey is confidence. Without confidence, you will have a difficult time getting team members to do what you need them to do. You can learn to read other's confidence levels, but the first person you must analyze is you. Are you portraying confidence as you sit, stand, and walk?

I mentioned before how it was pointed out to Matt that he was slumped over when he sat. It was also pointed out to him that his legs were crossed at his ankles and his arms were often crossed. This type of body position tells people whether they know it or not, that you are in a defensive or closed off position. When you are in this type of position, you are not portraying confidence. I will include a link in the resources section so you can see exactly what this looks like. Let me show you how to do this within minutes.

There are a few things you can do to immediately increase your confidence and how your confidence is viewed by others. This is based on scientific research from Amy Cuddy, a Ph.D. professor at Harvard Business School. Let's look at Matt's body position. I mentioned his arms and ankles were crossed. So if you were to coach Matt, the first thing you would tell him to do is uncross his arms and ankles.

By uncrossing your limbs, you open yourself up. When you are more open, you are viewed as more trusting. According to Cuddy, when people meet someone for the first time, they are evaluating two things. The first is, are they trustworthy. The second is, are they confident or competent. As I mentioned, by opening yourself up, you automatically adds a layer of trustworthiness in comparison to someone who has a body position that is closed off. Being open also sets off signals that you are confident. This is because someone who is confident doesn't need to be hiding behind anything or protecting themselves from anyone. After all, they are confident in who they are and what they are doing.

So if you were in a meeting with Matt, and you saw him sitting in one of the two positions I've mentioned, which one would you trust more and think is more confident or competent? Think about someone you've been around or have worked with a similar posture. Do they come across as trustworthy or confident? Are they able to command attention or influence those around them? Why is this important to you as a project manager?

As we previously talked about, your self-awareness is an important key to increasing your EQ. However, being aware of others' body language may also give you some insight into other people you work with and know how effective they can be as a member of your team. Not only that, but this will provide a path for you to know how to engage with each individual. Let's look at an example.

Let's say I am working with an engineer on a project, and I see that he is sitting similar to Matt, with arms and legs crossed. Also, I may notice that he often doesn't look up or into my eyes when he speaks. If you were to start speaking to him like a person with high confidence, you may cause him to shut down. For instance, if there is a task that is needed to be done and you approach this person aggressively, which a confident person would have little issue with because they would most likely respond to you with similar aggression, they may do what you need them to do but in the process they may lose respect for you. While some project managers may not initially care about losing respect, as long as what they need gets done, this could impede future progress as the project and team build momentum. As a project manager, the last thing you want to do is slow your project team's momentum. So how would you approach a person like this? Let's talk through one way to do this.

For someone who lacks confidence or is more closed off, we can make a few assumptions. One assumption is that they are not comfortable talking with others. You will find varying degrees of this in the workplace, but the simplest way to allow someone to open up is find out what their interests are. I don't mean their work or career interests but their personal interests. Yes, that's right; you are going to have to get personal. You can do this by simply taking a look at their desk and what they choose to display. What's at their desk is an indicator of what they are open to talking about.

For instance, if they have pictures of their children, take some time to ask about them. What are their names? What grade are they in? Do they have any hobbies? This may seem very basic, but you'd be surprised how many project managers, even the most experienced, bypass this step altogether and get to the action items. Taking the time to get to know the people on your team and understand what motivates them can be a first step to helping make your project run more smoothly. Further, if you can start to learn what their body language is saying, you can be better prepared to engage with your team and put yourself in a position to build strong relationships. In the process, you will be increasing your EQ not only in social awareness but also in relationship management, which we will talk about more later. Now that we've talked about self and social awareness, let's take a look at the management aspects of EQ – specifically self-management and relationship management.

Self-Management

So what is self-management, and why is it important to us as project managers? As a project manager, you are held responsible and accountable for how a project runs and its outcomes. In essence, you are the one throat to choke when it comes to the project. While it is true that the project manager is not the one solely responsible for the success or failure of a project, stakeholders will almost always look to you when things are going wrong. Typically, you won't be doing any of the programming or building of the product, but your stakeholders will look to you to answer for and be accountable for the good and the bad that happens during all phases of the project. Because of this, there are often a lot of stressful situations that occur during a project. How you manage these situations and, more importantly, how you manage yourself can make the difference between the success and failure of the project and whether you are awarded more projects in the future.

Where do you start when it comes to self-management? We previously talked about triggers. Once you understand what your triggers are, you must learn how to react to those triggers. This is where self-management comes in. The first thing to do is begin to keep a journal. You can't management something you're not aware of. Taking the time to list out your triggers may seem like a waste of time to some, but once you know what makes you stressed, angry, or excited, you can manage those emotions more effectively.

In its simplest form, you can see a low EQ and low self-management when watching a toddler throw a tantrum. Can you think of a time when you were working with or around someone who reacted like a toddler throwing a tantrum? I can tell you I have and I'll a share a very specific story with you.

During one of my projects, there was a technical issue that occurred, and one of the engineers on my project, Charlie, was not able to fix the problem and needed to do some more troubleshooting. This issue was on the laptop of an executive. Charlie came to me with a look a fear on his face and said the customer wanted to see me. I knew this couldn't be good, given the look on Charlie's face when he came in. So, Charlie and I got in the elevator and head up to the 21st floor. This executive had a host of initials after his name, including VP and MD, so he was very important, or so he thought he was. Unfortunately, for us, he was also known for his lack of people skills. As we entered his office, I greeted him and asked him what the problem was and how I could help resolve it immediately. He proceeded to tell me how he was late for his next meeting and could not get a report to work properly. The more he spoke and described his problem, the more red his face became, and the louder his voice got. After several minutes he began pounding his fists on the table, yelling at us that this needed to be fixed now and made several threats for added measure. As if that wasn't bad enough, he abruptly stood up, sending his chair flying into the wall behind him, creating a loud bang as he stomped out of the room to attend his next very important meeting. Stunned, Charlie and I just sat there staring at each other in disbelief. Just then his admin, an older woman with a very calming voice and look on her face, walked into the room and said, "don't worry boys he's not mad at you." Ha, you could have fooled us, I thought.

Luckily for Charlie and I, the whole situation happened so fast that neither of us had time to react. A reaction, of any kind, may have had a not so favorable outcome. So why would someone at such a high level with obviously a high degree of education, given the number of initials after his name, act that way? He was an intelligent and well-educated individual, but he clearly displayed a very low EQ in our brief encounter with him.

The bottom line is he did not know how to self-manage and was clearly not aware of his triggers. If he was self-aware, he chose to ignore his triggers. Now you may not experience this type of interaction during your career, and quite frankly, I hope you never do, but you will be tested. There are going to be those people that push your buttons. Your success will not come from just managing them, but more of it will come from how you manage yourself when you're dealing with these stressful situations. This brings me to my next point with self-management, and that is self-control.

Self-Control

As I mentioned, you are going to be tested. Having the self-control to not react the way you feel is critical. You may be thinking this is quite obvious, but consider our VP friend Charlie, and I encountered. You would think that someone with his pedigree and position would have his stuff together, but he didn't. You have to remember that in the work environment, people are under varying amounts of stress. Depending on the level of stress and their level EQ, will depend on how they react. The important thing to remember is that it's not about how they react but about how you react. You can only control person, and that is you. Let's look at a few specific ways you can increase your self-control.

Look at the big picture

As project managers, it can be very easy for us to get into the weeds, and most of us do. While it may be necessary to dive down into the minutia, it is not a place where we are meant to stay long term. You will need to look at and understand the bigger picture. Ask yourself, what part does this situation play in the bigger picture? Is this something that can affect the outcome of the project, or do you simply need to deal with the situation and move on? Clearly, understanding this will allow you to have a better perspective and allow you to manage the situation and yourself.

Relax and Stop

When you are in the throes of a big project, and the tension is mounting, it is important to relax and just stop to take a breath. The reason this is so important is that the act of stopping will help you avoid making impulse decisions. Too often, people in high-pressure situations react or make decisions impulsively. They see and feel the need to show a sense of urgency and dive headlong into a decision that could have catastrophic effects on the overall project. However, if you take the time to relax and think you decrease the chances you will overreact. So, how do you do this?

One of the simplest ways to employ a technique called box breathing. To do this, you will want to find a quiet place where you can comfortably sit. Next, close your eyes and breath in for 4 seconds. From here, you will want to hold your breath for 4 seconds. Then, you will exhale for 4 seconds. Finally, you will hold your breath for another 4 seconds. Once you've completed this last breath hold, you will start the process over by breathing in for 4 seconds and so on. Do this as many times as it takes for you to start to feel more relaxed. When you first start this exercise, you may feel slightly dizzy. This may be because you are not used to taking the time get that much oxygen into your system. I suggest you do this just once or twice at first to start so you can practice and be aware of how your body is reacting. It is also important to breathe through your abdomen instead of your chest. This will allow for deeper breathing and a more calming effect.

Why does this work? Without getting too scientific, this type of breathing activates your parasympathetic nervous system, which helps your body control things like digestion and lowers your heart rate, for example. These two things occur when you are in a more relaxed state and not preparing for fight or flight

Sleep

A lot of project managers spend countless hours, and many an overnighter, working and deploying their projects. However, without adequate sleep, your decision-making and self-control will suffer. I do want to make sure you understand the part sleep plays in your ability to control yourself and your emotions. Look again at the toddler example. If you've ever been around a toddler when they are approaching their bedtime, you will see a sweet and loving child turn into a little demon, almost as if watching a werewolf transform, as the full moon appears. You don't want to be that person, so make sure you get enough sleep.

Self-Discipline

Another aspect of self-management is self-discipline. Whether you are new project management or have been managing projects for several years, you already know how easy it is to get distracted. At work, you have people stopping by your desk, phone ringing, email, instant messenger, and so on. This doesn't include the number personal distractions like texts and social media. The number of distractions is endless. One of the things you have to get really good at is self-discipline. As professionals, we know this, but knowing and putting it into action are two completely different things. Since most projects have so many variables going on, it's easy to get distracted with the issue of the day. Let's look at a few ways you can improve your self-discipline.

Start Small

When looking to change a habit, it is often best to go for the low hanging fruit. You know those things that are easiest to tackle? I don't know about you, but I get hundreds of emails every day. Some are important for me to react and respond to immediately, but most of them I am simply copied on, so I am kept in the loop. This was a source of distraction for me and one I needed to learn to manage. Now I will admit, I am still a work in progress when it comes to email, but I'm definitely much better than I used to be. Several years ago, I found myself spending hours each day reading, thinking about, and responding to emails. So much so that it was starting to affect my work output and focus. So I decided to make some adjustments, and I can tell you the benefits have given me back several hours during my week. What I did was keep my email off and only checked it during certain times of the day. This way, I was controlling the flow of information versus reacting when something came in. I'm not dealing with life and death situations, so I did not have to worry about being on call every minute. This freed me up to do the things I need to do to make progress on my project. The caveat to this email strategy is it did take me some time to get over the addiction of having to check email all the time. Email, for a lot of people, gives them a sense of importance and something to occupy their time.

The reality is very few people really need to be available for every email that comes in on a second by second basis. Over time, I was able to create the self-discipline to check my email during certain times of the day. Even though this adjustment was very small, it paid off in big dividends when it came to my time. So pick something you can you can adjust that is small and manageable before you start tackling the big stuff.

Get Focused

We've already talked about the number of distractions we encounter during our day, so getting and staying focused is extremely important. However, I'm not talking about being focused for hours at a time. Quite frankly, very few can do that. What I'm talking about is a short burst of effort using what is known as the Pomodoro Technique. According to Wikipedia, "the Pomodoro Technique is a time management method developed by Francesco

Cirillo in the late 1980s. The technique uses a timer to break down work into intervals, traditionally 25 minutes in length, separated by short breaks. These intervals are named *Pomodoros*." There are a number of timers you can download from your app store or by searching on Google. You can even just set a timer on your phone for 25 minutes and use that. I'll be sure to include resources on this topic.

One of the key aspects of this technique is to remove all distraction and only focus on the task at hand for 25 minutes. Shutting down your email for this short time will help. Do you think you and your world can survive without you checking email for 25 minutes? This focused attention does two main things:

1) The most obvious is it leaves you free of distraction so you can get more done during those 25 minutes
2) when you give yourself only 25 minutes to finish something the sense of urgency is

increased. This allows you to tap into your creativity and bring more of the best out of you because you only have a short period of time in which to accomplish your task.

So, if you want to be more self-disciplined, get more focused in short bursts.

Fail

Okay, this one may seem counter-intuitive. After all, the last thing you want to do as a project manager is fail. What do I mean by this? I mean, don't fear failure. With the Pomodoro Technique, I described, there are some that won't even try because they are afraid, they will fail to complete the task in the allotted time. So instead of taking the risk, they never start.

A common trait I've noticed among many project managers, and most people in general, is their adversity to failure. Most view failure as a bad thing when, in fact, it's not. As a matter of fact, failure is critical to success. Why is this?

The simple reason is when you fail; you are typically at the out edge of your skill set or comfort zone. Identifying these edges allows you to learn more and grow.

If you are able to view failure as an opportunity to improve, you will conclude that the more and faster you fail, the more and faster you will improve. Fear of failure is often seen among project managers when reporting status. Many are afraid to report a failure, a miss, or a shortcoming on a project because they fear it will be a reflection on them. I used to do this myself. I'd try to paint a rosy picture on the front end while I frantically worked on the back end to fix the problem so nobody would know.

What I didn't realize was that not reporting the miss, issue, or risk was an opportunity to communicate to those that could possibly help. In my want to not fail or look incompetent, I was missing out on creating alliances with the very people that could make my life easier and help make the project successful. So if you want more self-discipline learn to not be afraid of failure.

You know yourself better than anybody, so you can probably come up with several more ways to be more self-disciplined. I encourage you to take the time to develop this aspect of self-management, and you will see the positive effects in a short period of time.

Self-Talk

This topic may sound strange to you when it comes to project management, but the reality is that what we say to ourselves on a daily basis has a profound effect on how we perform. This isn't some woo-woo pseudo-scientific nonsense. Your self-talk creates physical and neurological changes in your brain. For instance, if you have had negative self-talk for several years, then you are reinforcing the grooves in your brain that support this type of thinking. The same goes with the positive thoughts. When you attempt to change your self-talk, you are creating new patterns and connections in your brain. Consequently, you are creating new pathways, much like cars driving down a new dirt road. Over time, grooves will be formed on this road with every passing car.

Think back to the last encounter you had with someone. It could have been a hallway conversation, a status meeting, or even just a meet with friends outside of work. I will bet that prior to or during that conversation, you were saying things to yourself. Let me give you an example.

Early in my career, I was given the opportunity to take over a project that wasn't going so well. I was new to project management, and the person I was taking over for was much more experienced than I was. I had all sorts of doubts and thoughts running through my head as I started to work on this project. I remember thinking things like; I don't have enough experience, and what if I fail? Is anybody going to listen to me? What if I screw up? What if I disappoint my boss? The list went on and on. Have you had similar thoughts?

What I didn't realize then was that these thoughts, while some being very valid, were not helping me move forward. This self-talk was never going to get me to a place where I could perform at my best. If I were to go back to young Bryan and give him some advice in this area, I would say three things:

1) Become self-aware. Sound familiar? The first thing I'd do is to become aware of my self-talk. What am I saying to myself? We all talk to ourselves, so it's not like you have to go far or dig deep to simply be aware. Like we've talked about, being aware of what you are doing and saying is part of your emotional intelligence. With this first point, you are just observing. There is no judgment. Your self-talk just is what it is and nothing more. Your job in this step is to identify what you are saying to yourself and write it down.

2) Modify any negative self-talk to something more positive and in a way that will move you forward. For example, if you say to yourself, "I'm not a good public speaker," then change this to "When I speak, people are interested in what I want to hear." Does this mean that once you start saying this that people will want to hear what you have to say? No, they won't. However, over time, your belief will cause you to act differently. This change is what will cause people to be interested in what you have to say. Your body language will change, your voice tone, inflection, and volume will change. All the components that would make you someone people want to listen to you will start come through. The reason for this is our subconscious mind is like a heat-seeking missile. It cannot tell between reality and imaginary. If you tell your brain something it will start to work to prove that right. The rational part of our brain that tells us what is real or imagined is our conscious mind. Don't believe me? Think back to a movie that had a sad or scary part in it. Did you cry or

were you scared? Was what was going on in the movie real? Of course not, but you still reacted. If the movie was sad you may have cried. Was there any logical reason for you to cry? Your subconscious brain was reacting to the imagined scenario presented in the movie. Likewise, we can begin to create our own reality by changing what we say to ourselves.

3) The final step is repetition. Your thought processes and habits have come from years and years of self-talk. It will take time for these new pathways and connections to develop. I've read that it takes 21 days to create a habit. However, after doing a lot of research, I discovered it takes a little bit longer than that. If you are going to make a lasting change, I would suggest repeating whatever self-talk you choose for 60 days. The longer you repeat your message, the deeper the grooves in your brain will become, and the longer the thought process will last. Eventually, repeated enough times, the new thought pattern will become how you

automatically think. Depending on where you are, your background, and your current self-talk, it may take more than 60 days. My recommendation is you do it long enough until your self-talk has changed without you having to consciously think about it. Just start with one message at first. Remember, start small. Now that you've started to improve your self-talk it's time to take a look at another aspect of self-management, and that is your habits.

Habits

For this portion of the book, I'd like to share an excerpt from my first book on Habits. You will see that your habits tie directly into what we discussed about self-discipline.

How often do we know what's good for us, yet we fail to act? The discipline of acting on what we know to be true, rather than what we feel, helps tackle the uncertainties of life. Growing up, it seemed that most of my decisions were rooted in reacting inappropriately to my emotions—doing what I felt instead of doing what I knew I should do.

At the time I started college in Southern California, I was an avid surfer and loved my time at the beach. I distinctly remember driving up the freeway to get to class, getting off the exit, and at the stop light, I was faced with a decision. Do I go left, or do I go, right? You see, the class was to my right, and the beach was to my left. I always had my surfboard with me, so I didn't have to worry about heading back home. How convenient was that? Do you think I planned to go surfing the whole time even though my intention was to go to class? Needless to say, my grades that semester were average at best, but it didn't stop there. I took the habit of doing what I felt into my work life. If there was a hard task in front of me, I would procrastinate and work on something easier until right before the hard task was due. Then I'd scurry around frantically trying to get my assignment completed. In hindsight, I see that this unhealthy behavior was really a lack of discipline.

A 2013 study by Wilhelm Hoffman, a professor at the University of Cologne, showed that people with high self-control or people that do what they know are happier than those without. People with strong self-discipline tend to not waste time on behaviors that are detrimental to their wellness and instead practice healthy habits in their daily routine. Rather than allowing limiting emotions or impulses to dictate their behavior, they remain committed to the disciplines that they had thoughtfully formulated were good for their overall health and success. Though self-discipline can be difficult to learn, it is, in fact, a learned behavior that can be developed over time.

As you can see, there are several components to self-management, but once you have established a strong foundation for managing yourself, you will notice that not only have you changed, but others around you will have changed in the way they work and deal with you. This goes hand in hand with the final component of a project manager's emotional intelligence, and that is Relationship Management.

Relationship Management

As a project manager, your project will live and die by the relationships you are able to create and maintain. In this section, we will discuss some strategies you can implement to not only increase your EQ but solidify your relationships and ensure the success of your project.

Be Interested

A lot of project managers I've come in contact with spend more time being interested in what they want for themselves. Unfortunately, what they want is not always what will make the project move forward or influence others to do what the project manager wants. If you want to build relationships with your stakeholders and your teams, you must first be interested in them. Let's first start with your stakeholders.

Your stakeholders are the ones paying for your project, so to not take the time to fully understand what they want is like preparing to deliver something they don't need or want. Understanding what they want starts with first understanding them, their role, their temperament, and perhaps some of their long-term objectives for the project and their own career. If you have not worked with these stakeholders, the first thing to do is to start to build trust. The only way they will trust you, without you having delivered anything, is if they get to know you and like you. Until you can prove you are able to deliver, this is all they have to go on. So, if you're interested in building trust and building a relationship with your stakeholders, you must first be interested in them.

Building a relationship with your team is very similar to your stakeholder, in that you need to build trust with them. Because of your position as the project manager, there will be a certain amount of built-in trust. However, you will have those that don't trust anyone until they prove themselves. In either case, like with your stakeholders, you must first get to know them, and they must grow to like you if you are going to get them to fully trust you. Can you successfully complete a project without your team liking and trusting you? Sure, you can. However, your life will be much easier if they like and trust you as you will have more influence over them. In his book, *Influence: The Psychology of Persuasion*, one of Robert Cialdini's pillars of influence is likability. He states, "Few people would be surprised to learn that as a rule, we most prefer to say yes to the requests of someone we know and like. What might be startling to note, however, is that this simple rule is used in hundreds of ways by total strangers to get us to comply with their requests." If this is true, and I believe it is, how much more can you get done, and how many more people can you influence if you improve your likability?

Depending on the industry you are in, you may not have dedicated resources. In other words, the resources assigned to your project may also have duties on other projects, which mean that you may not always be their top priority. One of the keys to your success as a project manager is to make your project the number one priority in the minds of your team. One of the best ways to do this is to create a relationship with them and grow that relationship so they like and trust you more than other project managers, whose time you will be competing with. If you are fortunate enough to have dedicated resources working on your project, then so much the better. However, if you are going to get the most out of your team, build strong relationships by being interested in them.

Care About Your Team

One of my favorite quotes is by Theodore Roosevelt, and he said, "People don't care how much you know until they know how much you care." Through the years, many people have quoted these words, but the truth remains that if you want people to care how much you know, you are going to need to care about them first.

In our world of deadlines, instant gratification, and short attention spans, most are used to just moving through their day at a fast and hectic pace. Especially for those of us who are project managers, we have to deliver on time and on budget, so we have to drive, drive, drive. Right? Well, yes, we do. However, it doesn't mean we can't take the time to care about our team.

I have worked with some amazing project managers whose care meter is off the charts. It's the little things. For instance, for every early morning meeting they have, they bring donuts. During team meetings, they individually recognize the efforts of those going above and beyond. If something is going on, personally, with a member of their team, they take the time to ask and show genuine concern. All these actions are not done out of wanting to manipulate anyone. They do these things because it is who they are at their core.

I will never forget a project I was working on, not as a project manager, but as a technical resource. We had had a long night of installation and troubleshooting, and the team was tired. The next day, I had a card on my desk with a note that read, "Thank you for doing more than what's expected." Nobody else ever said anything about the work that was done, but that simple gesture made the hours and effort worth it. I will tell you that anytime this project manager needed anything, I was willing and ready. Feeling cared for is a basic human need. Give it freely, and it will pay dividends when it comes to building relationships.

Be Empathetic

Empathy has always been interesting to me. At our core, many of us just want to be understood. As teenagers, we go through this because we don't think our parents or the world understands us. When we get into the workforce, empathy has a way of getting lost. It's those that can show empathy that stands out.

Understanding someone's feelings takes time and effort to understand. Remember, I mentioned how you will have resources where your project is not the only project they are working on? Understanding their situation when they have two or more project managers vying for their attention can go a long way. One thing that I've seen work well is taking some of the burdens from them by talking to the other project manager and working through any scheduling conflicts. First, however, ask the resource if this is something, they would be ok with you doing on their behalf. Most of the time, you are not their direct manager, so some may take offense to your managing their time outside of your project. However, if you talk to them first and show them that you understand the situation they are in, they may be more than willing to have you work things out for them. This can go a long way in building a strong relationship with that individual.

Stakeholder Management

We've taken some time to talk about relationship management as it relates to your team. Now let's take a look at your stakeholders and how you can build and manage these relationships. According to pmi.org, "Successful projects depend upon a variety of people, and it is the wise project manager who actively determines who they are and what areas of the project they influence. A forgotten stakeholder often rears his or her head at the most inopportune time, wreaking all sorts of havoc in the project. But many project teams do a poor job of identifying project stakeholders and gaining their commitment to the project."

Stakeholder management will utilize some of the skills we talked about earlier, but it will utilize several more skills that will benefit you in future leadership roles, should that be a path you decide to pursue. One such skill and probably one of the most important to any project manager and leader is communication.

Let's take a look at how to utilize effective communication to build stronger relationships.

Communication

Although the art and skill of effective communication are so critical to being an effective project manager and in relationship management, it is by far one of the most difficult skills to master. Why do you think this is so difficult?

There are probably hundreds of reasons why, but I will give you my opinion on this subject. My opinion has been formed over the past 20 years from, quite frankly, messing up A LOT in this area. To this day, I'm still learning and will continue to learn with every project I work on. So, what do I think the reason communication is so difficult? I believe it is because all of us spend most of our time thinking about ourselves. Yes, I know this is a bold statement to say all of us. But, think about this for a minute.

For the majority of the day, are you think about other people, or are you thinking about the things you need to do or getting lost in your own thoughts? You are thinking about you, right?

There is nothing wrong with this; in fact, this is how we are wired. From the time you were a baby, you were focused on your needs, being fed, changed, and cared for. As you grew up, you began to take care of those needs, but the needs remained the same. Throughout your day, you are planning what needs to be done or doing things you need to do. As a project manager, you're focused on getting the project completed as part of your job. As you do this, you are thinking of what you need to do. Again, none of this is wrong; it just is. Have you ever been in a conversation where you were trying to think of the next thing to say to the person you were talking to, instead of really listening to what they were saying? I know I have, many times.

In my case, because I was focused on what I was going to say next, I wasn't really listening. My focus and attention were on my next brilliant statement. If you were to ask a group of adults what they thought one of the most important parts of communication is, I think most would agree that listening would be at or near the top of the list. If you are going to be strong at relationship management, you are going to have to become very strong in the art and skill of communication. The first step to being a strong communicator is to become a great listener.

Listening is not just hearing what they say, but it's also observing what they don't say. Take the scenario I will describe in the diplomacy section. You will learn that Tom, a vendor I was engaged to work with, was telling me he wanted to make sure he was brought in and contacted first before anyone came on site. As I listened to his voice, his tone and frustration said a lot more than that. He was looking to be supported, heard, and respected. When it comes to listening, what people don't say is almost more important than what they do say. Take the time to improve your listening skills by using some the techniques below.

Do:

- Maintain eye contact
- Be present
- Ask questions to gain understanding
- Provide feedback
- Be open minded

Don't:

- Look at your phone or computer
- Interrupt

So why are there more Do's than don'ts on the list above? The reality is that for every Don't, there are several Do's. I want you to focus more on the Do's as you develop your listening skills. This is not an exhaustive list, but you can find many more resources out there on how to be an effective listener. I recommend you take the time to actively study this topic.

Since communication is such a key component to building and maintaining relationships, let's look at a few more aspects of communication beyond listening.

No Surprises

Since communication is vital, it is important to communicate both the good and that bad news. In each project you work on, there will be something that will come up that is unexpected. In the case where you need to deliver news about a delay or change, it is better to give your stakeholders early notice. While they may be disappointed, letting them know early is much better than having to tell them after the delay has happened. Worse yet, they find out through other sources. Let's look at an example that Matt dealt with.

It was around mid-year, and Matt found out that, through one of his vendors, that over half of the equipment he was expecting to be delivered was going to be delayed by several months. This was something that was completely out of Matt's control, and he had no alternative but to adjust the current schedule. His planned go-live date was the end of the year, but after adjusting the schedule due to the delays, this was going to push out the go-live date to the end of the first quarter of the following year.

As soon as he had the new dates, he walked over to his stakeholder's office to let them know the news. While they were not happy to hear about the delay and questioned Matt on other alternatives and possible mitigation, they understand that Matt had done all he could to deliver the solution as soon as possible. Matt made sure to document their discussion then let his team and any other parties that needed to know about the delay.

In this scenario, while quite simplistic, Matt did not delay or hesitate in letting his stakeholder know what was going on as soon as possible. By doing this, he did two main things. 1) He didn't allow his stakeholder to be surprised by the "bad news" 2) By letting the stakeholder know early, he gave his stakeholder the opportunity to help come up with a solution while there was still time. One of my biggest learnings early on in my career was how to handle the delivery of bad news. Unfortunately, I learned this the hard way by doing the exact opposite of what Matt did, and that is to wait to communicate. What I did instead was try to fix the problem on my own, in a vacuum, and delayed telling my stakeholders what was going on. I did this because I was scared of their reaction or that I might get in trouble. The reality is, as a project manager, it is your job to report the good, the bad, and the ugly – and as soon as possible. You are not out to win a popularity contest. Where I was afraid of getting in trouble for delivering some not so favorable information, I was actually risking a greater wrath by delaying the inevitable.

Communicating often and early is vital to the success of your project. While you may be the bearer of bad news at times, you are the lead communicator for your team. So, take the necessary steps, and make sure all who need to know know early and often.

Diplomacy

According to dictionary.com, the definition of diplomacy is the "skill in managing negotiations, handling people, etc., so there is little or no ill will." Let me share a quick story to illustrate this definition.

Recently I received an email from a vendor partner which simply stated, "Please call me." Remember, I mentioned Tom? I really didn't think anything of it as we are always talking about different project related items. When we got on the phone, he started to tell me about another vendor who took it upon themselves to come to the location, where he was the site manager, and started looking around so they could get some measurements for a deployment we were working on. Well, the site manager, Tom, did not appreciate someone coming on-site without notice.

As we spoke, Tom's voice started to escalate as he relayed the story to me. He said that he is in charge of the site and that if anyone needs to see anything, they need to go through him. The more he talked, the more charged up he got. At this point, all I could do was listen. He had a valid point, but he wanted me to go talk to the other vendor and let them know the rules. Because I needed both to work together, I needed to act quickly and make sure Tom got what he needed, which was to be validated and feel supported. I also needed to make sure that my other vendor understood the ground rules of the engagement at that particular site.

I called the offending vendor and explained the rules of engagement at that site. In doing so, I needed to make sure I maintained a good relationship with him since we were coming close to the deadline of the critical milestones, and any delays or hiccups could cause the project to go beyond our expected schedule. Although a minor incident, if not handled properly, a situation like this could have escalated to a point where it affected not only the working relationship of the vendors but could have posed a serious threat to the overall schedule and project completion.

If you want to be effective as a project manager, you will need to include diplomacy in your overall education on emotional intelligence.

Conclusion

So where do you go from here? You've been armed with quite a bit of knowledge on emotional intelligence, and it can be quite daunting to understand the path to take so you get the most benefit from what you've learned. As I look back on my career, and if I were to go back to my younger self, I would advise focusing first on self-awareness. When you are new to project management, you have so many things to focus on and learn. The technical aspects alone can be daunting. Then you add the soft skills, and it is easy to understand why the field of project management is so complex and lucrative.

As you develop your technical skills also take the time to understand who you are as a person and as a project manager. This can be done via the approach I have outlined, by assessing yourself, having others assess you, and find a formal assessment. Also, as I mentioned previously, understand what your triggers are. You would be surprised at that number of people that are in constant reaction mode simply because they do not understand their own triggers.

If you want to be a great project manager, make the time to learn some of the skills you've been taught in this book. Also, utilize some the resources in the next few pages to further your education. I think you will find that increasing your Emotional Intelligence will pay you dividends for years to come. I wish you the best of luck on your project management and Emotional Intelligence journey.

Resources

EQ Books

Emotional Intelligence 2.0

by Travis Bradberry – includes assessment code

Emotional Intelligence: Why It Can Matter More Than IQ

by Daniel Goleman

Confidence video by Amy Cuddy

Pomodoro Timer – Type in Pomodoro in your phone's app store or go here

HABITS:

CREATE WHAT YOU NEED TO SUCCEED IN LIFE

By

Bryan Oliver

Why You Should Read This Book

The following pages are home to time-tested habits whose intended audience is recent college graduates and those who are early in their career. However, the habits discussed are not time sensitive, so they can be mastered regardless of what stage in life you may find yourself in. Each chapter contains an explanation of the habit followed by a Reality Check. This is designed to give real world examples of how these habits were applied to my life and the lives of others. These habits are interrelated and provide a powerful foundation for your future endeavors. Learning to create strong and healthy habits is not only essential, but it is the fundamental difference between those who achieve their goals and those who provide excuses. This book is more than just my experiences; it is the culmination of relationships I've built for 18 years with people ranging from wide-eyed students to experienced executives. However, like a horse taken to water, the choice is and always will be yours to take action.

In this book, you will learn ten habits to help reframe your mindset and move you forward in a short and easy to read format. Learn one or all ten; again, the choice is yours. Nevertheless, prepare yourself to create habits that will help you succeed in life.

Habit # 1: Surround yourself with healthy, like-minded people

Consider this: The five people you spend the most time with have the highest potential to shape your future. Now stop for a moment and think about who you hang out with. Who are you surrounded by at school or work? Your friends and colleagues subconsciously affect several areas of your life, including the income you make, where you live, and even your health. I am not suggesting getting rid of your friends, but if you are not at a place where you want to be or at least headed in that direction, I suggest that you sit down and evaluate what you want your life to look like in five, ten, and twenty years. Are the people in your life helping you move toward or away from those goals? Some tough decisions may need to be made with regard to your sphere of influence.

Think about some of the habits you currently have—good or bad—and see if those are similar to some of the people you are surrounded by. Are they helping you move forward in life, or are they holding you back? While there are some people you will need to steer clear of; you can start influencing your peers with some of the habits you've learned thus far. You'll be surprised how quickly they notice a change in you. I recommend that you seek out a mentor who is at a place where you want to be. Most successful people didn't get to where they are alone. They surrounded themselves with healthy, like-minded people that challenged them to be better and guide them on the journey toward success. They also understand that they have a responsibility to pay that forward. Likewise, it will be your responsibility to groom and shape our future generations as you achieve success.

Reality Check

When I first started my career, I met someone who greatly influenced my future. His name was Joe. Although we were about the same age, he owned a house, drove a luxury car without a car payment, and had no credit card debt. I, on the other hand, lived in an apartment, drove an okay car with a car payment, and had a large amount of debt.

One day, I asked Joe how he got to be where he was at such a young age. He was more than willing to share, and this is what he told me. He said when he was in high school, his friends called him "Lunch Box Joe." Each day his parents would give him lunch money for school, but Joe would save his lunch money and pack a lunch box. Between working part-time and saving his lunch money, he was able to buy his first house at the age of 18.

I was shocked. I couldn't figure out whether I wanted to go to the beach or watch television at

18, let alone decide and afford to buy a house. Over the next several years, I got to see how Joe acted and the choices he made. He read a lot and listened to positive and transformational recordings every chance he got—especially in the car. The most important things I learned from him were the habits and discipline it took to achieve the level of success Joe achieved. He didn't have more talent or opportunity than I did, but he had reached a level of success that I never thought was possible.

Today, Joe continues to be grounded and happy with a wonderful family. He is an executive at a large international company, lives in a beautiful home that he paid for in cash, and still has no debt. I am grateful to Joe for showing me how to think and act differently.

I have been fortunate to be surrounded by people, younger and older, who are a positive influence and teach me every day. Over the last 15 years, I have been very selective with whom I spend my time with because as positive as someone can be to move me forward, the wrong person can have an equally negative affect on your life. Be selective and protect you and your family's future. If you do not already have someone in your life that is where you want to be, go find your Joe. You will become a different person in the process.

Habit #2: Provide value

Hard work is essential and imperative to get ahead, but it will only get you so far. Beyond that, you have to create value that is worth more to your employer and customer than they perceive they are paying for. Value is realized when the worth or usefulness of something becomes self-evident and sought after.

Early in life, to build self-esteem, we are told we receive an A for effort. While that is effective in early childhood development, that mentality alone will not produce value as an adult—especially in the business world. In the business world, you must provide greater value than your competition, all of the time. This is true in calculating measurable or perceived value.

Let's review measurable value first. Imagine a lovable coworker that everyone enjoys being around. They brighten the office with their demeanor and are encouraging to all. They treat people with dignity and respect and are fun to be around. In immeasurable ways, they add value to the office, making their perceived value is high. However, if the same person habitually fails to produce results, they're often late or are unprepared for meetings, their measurable value is considerably low.

Another perspective is perhaps you've worked with someone who produces excellent results and is at the top of their game. Their numbers are stellar and continue to trend upward. However, they are difficult to work with and often enable unnecessary conflict amongst the team. Not interested in building team cohesiveness, they focus solely on getting themselves ahead. This behavior makes them valuable for little other than the results they produce. While their measurable value is high, their perceived value is low.

Many new to the workforce are eager to please, but as the novelty fades, maintaining the pursuit of excellence can be more challenging. This ultimately causes some to become complacent. It takes emotional maturity, stamina, and drive to get to a point where providing value becomes a habit. Providing value is something that must consciously be on the forefront of your mind and must be practiced in order to be successful in your career.

How do you know if you're providing perceived and/or measurable value? The answer is simple: All one has to do is ask. Asking your manager, peers, clients, or even those outside of your business relationships can piece together a mirror for you to view your measurable and perceived value. Part of your growth will come from having the emotional maturity to receive criticism and look for ways to increase your perceived value.

Perceived value is never more apparent than in the job interview process. In this process, your measurable value is tenuous at best because the evaluation and decision is based on brief interactions. While education and experience listed on a resume may get you an interview, the perceived value of how you answer to situational and cultural scenarios plays a vital role in the final hiring decision. Creating habits that add to your overall success, like providing perceived value, will go a long way toward increasing your value and, ultimately, your net worth in the marketplace.

Reality Check

If you've recently graduated from college and are just getting started in your career, you may think it will take some time before you can add significant value to your company. Let me tell you about Asma. Asma joined our firm straight out of college. Shy in nature, she was extremely smart and eager to make a change. She began her career in an entry level position and was excited to have her first job right out of college. After just a few months, she started to notice there were other colleagues that had similar questions as she did. She was learning a lot from the leaders in the firm, and she, along with her peers, wanted to know what it would take to become a leader. Like an antenna, she was constantly tuned in for advice from leaders around her, and she soon began to implement that advice in her daily life. To ensure results, she sought immediate feedback, so she knew she was on the right track.

Shortly thereafter, Asma had an epiphany; what if a program was created for young consultants to learn leadership skills that are used in business every day? She began to put the pieces together for this program to present the idea to the managing partners of the firm. For Asma, it wasn't enough to just have a good idea. She needed to show what value this would bring to individuals in the program, clients, and the firm. She came up with a proposal, presented it, and it was accepted.

In addition to her day job, she began to design the program. Working with the leaders of our firm to understand the needs of our clients and her peers, Asma created a program that we now call our Emerging Leaders Program, or ELP for short. In addition to this, she leads and was instrumental in the design of our internship program. She has provided significant value to our clients, our firm, and for those individuals that are part of the EL and Internship programs.

Consider this: Asma saw a need and took action on something that she thought would provide value. She consulted with experts in her field so she could create a program that would grow beyond her own efforts. The leaders that come out of this program will have a lasting impact on hundreds, if not thousands, of individuals in the years to come. The measurable value Asma brought was creating and driving the ELP and internship programs. Her perceived value is that of a trusted advisor and contributor who will continue to provide measurable value in the future. What value are you providing to your company and to your clients?

Habit #3: Do more than what's expected

If you are going to succeed in life and achieve anything of significance, you will need to do more than what's expected. Be prepared to be tired, work more hours than others, work with little to no recognition for your effort, and be prepared to stop focusing on what you want and instead focus on what other people want.

According to the founder of Mary Kay, "There are four kinds of people in the world: Those that make things happen, those who watch things happen, those that wonder what happened, and those that don't know that anything happened." Most people fall into the latter three categories. Since you are here to learn to create the habits to succeed, let's shine a light on the first kind of person.

Many people leave college expecting an exciting job that blossoms into a handsomely-paying career they will love for years to come. However, many recent graduates quickly become disillusioned when entry level jobs do not meet their expectations. The reality is that most recent college grads do not obtain their dream job right away. Instead, they work hard to build some experience and, if they're lucky, get their foot in the door and start building a career on the path to their dream job.

Let's take a look at the mindset above. What expectations does this person have? Are those expectations realistic? Throughout your career, significant focus should be placed on who you are becoming in addition to improving your skills and job performance. One way to improve job performance is by doing more than what's expected of you. I see too many people, both young and experienced, get caught up in only working toward a title and focusing on minimum requirements. I know this because not only have I seen it happen where I've worked, but I was once guilty of the same thought process—and I paid for it.

Avoid this cycle of mismanaging expectations by training yourself to do whatever is needed as often as needed and confirming what the given expectations are. Take it a step further by having the humility to work without recognition and do all things with integrity. Your ability to self-motivate during these times is what will set you apart from your peers. In order to be truly successful, you will have to do more than what is expected.

Reality Check

The summer after graduating from high school, I got a job at a surf shop in Newport Beach, California. On my breaks, I would go down the boardwalk to a local convenience store. Working there was a young man with Down syndrome named Charlie. Every day when I'd walk in, he'd say, "Hi Mr. Bryan! Are you having a great day?" I'd match his enthusiasm and energy and reply back with a smile on my face, "Yes, Charlie, it's a great day!" The greeting alone is not what made Charlie special. Not only did he make everyone that walked through the door feel important, he was always helping them find what they needed as if they were the only one in the world that mattered.

One day, in particular, I had come in as usual, and Charlie was helping a couple find what they needed. There was a specific suntan lotion they wanted but couldn't find. Overhearing the conversation, I leaned over and told Charlie that we carried that specific brand of suntan lotion at the surf shop where I worked. He smiled and disappeared from the store.

Both the couple and I just stood there and wondered where Charlie went. They resumed their shopping, and I did mine. Several minutes later, Charlie appeared and yelled, "I got it!" Everyone in the store looked over at him. In his hand was the bottle of suntan lotion the customer was looking for.

Instead of referring the customers to the surf shop to go buy the suntan lotion, he ran and purchased it himself so they wouldn't have to. The couple was very grateful, and you could see the look of pride on Charlie's face. Over the years. I've thought about Charlie and the lesson he taught me that day. Implementing the habit of doing more than what's expected can have a profound impact on the relationships you create and service you provide in your business.

Habit #4: Understand personality styles

This habit, above all others, has had the most profound effect on my career. Your personality—how you tend to think, feel, and behave—is shaped by your genetic makeup as well as your life experiences. Our personalities determine the way we interact with people in our life. Understanding the power of our personality will help prepare us to attain success.

Part of being a successful and competent individual in the workplace is knowing your strengths, weaknesses, communication, and learning styles. There are many excellent personality assessments that can assist you in discovering more about yourself. As you learn more about your own personality type, it is imperative that you learn more about the personality types of others.

There are four basic personalities. Depending on the personality test you take, the names may be different. The four main personality types are:

- Type A
- Analytical
- Feeler
- Expressive

People who are Type A tend to focus on fact rather than emotion. They are driven to see measurable results, and their intensity may make them quick to offend, even though that may not be their intention. Type A personalities like to act quickly and are enthusiastic about tackling projects and seeing results. If you want something done, call the Type A personality.

Analytical personalities like to amass details and comb through them first rather than acting hastily. They value accuracy in their work and expect the same precision and excellence from others. They relate to Ben Franklin's motto,

"Everything has a place and everything in its place."

People with Feeler personalities are people-centric and value meaningful relationships. This personality style makes for great team players, as these personalities are patient and seek to interact with their coworkers on a personal level. They are revealing when it comes to the events of their life, hope to know others, and are sensitive to the feelings of others. If you need someone to talk to, go find the Feeler personality. They can talk through issues with you and are willing to help if they can.

Those with Expressive personalities are creative and astute in the art of persuasion. Because they are enthusiastic and friendly, expressive personalities value communication with others and thrive when lines of communication are open. Expressive personalities long for recognition and often need support to reign in their many ideas in order to achieve specific goals.

It is important to remember that no one person fits perfectly into one category. Each individual is likely to express characteristics that are indicative to all four types, with a greater emphasis on one or two. These categories are not meant to put people into behavioral boxes. Instead, they are meant to help us better understand each other's tendencies. These characteristics can help understand the deeper motivations of each member on your team, including the most important person—yourself.

To understand your own personality and where you tend to lean, consider taking an in-depth personality test like Myers-Briggs or Strengthsfinder 2.0. Learning your personality type will be an ongoing process and study for the remainder of your career. Once you've gained a basic framework of your personality, the next step is to learn about the other three styles and how they work together. As a leader, you will need to understand your team's personality style and tendencies in order to place them in positions to achieve highest degree of success.

Reality Check

Earlier in my career, working extra hours wasn't hard because I was learning, and I enjoyed the mental stimulation. Knowing this, one of my earlier managers asked me if I'd be interested in being a lead for a particular project. I accepted, not realizing I had just changed the course of my career. In this project, I spent time with the project manager and began to become interested in what he did. Naturally, I asked a lot of questions, and he answered all of them happily. One evening, the project manager called in sick. Taking initiative, I asked him if I could run the team and act as project manager for the night. He agreed, and that night I took over all duties and work ran smoothly. The next day I revealed my experience to the project manager and let him know how much fun I had the night before. He gladly let me take over some of the responsibilities for the next several weeks. He monitored my work and reported the progress back to my manager.

One morning, my manager called me into his office and revealed that one of our star project managers had a failing project. He needed me to fly down to Pasadena, California, to help fix the problem. I was simultaneously excited and scared. I knew the project manager, and he was a strong Type A personality who commanded attention. Because I had been reading a lot of books and listening to motivational speakers, I knew I had to stretch myself if I was going to grow and advance. Off to Pasadena, I went.

Arriving in Pasadena, my manager called me and told me the truth of why I was there. The project manager in Pasadena was removed from the project because he had butted heads with the client. The truth was that not only did I need to complete the project, I also needed to fix the relationship with the client. My first meeting was with the head of the department. She was about 20 years my senior and very stoic. She revealed that due to the mishap of the other project manager, she wanted results, and she wanted them fast. She was definitely a Type A personality. I got the information I needed from her, clarified what she was looking for, and went on my way to produce the results.

One part of my responsibilities was to meet with each client during the day before the evening's activities. Some had very specific and detailed requirements, and others had to step into the process of what we were doing and assure them everything was going to be okay. Even still, others wanted to talk about everything under the sun regarding their job duties. Each user had their own unique set of needs, and I had to quickly learn to adapt to their concerns.

After gathering the necessary information and speaking to the clients, our team began performing. In order to make sure the customers had a smooth transition, I arrived at 7am after a full night of activities. I met each user as they walked in the door, walked them through their new system, and showed them where their files were. Some appreciated the efforts, and others didn't even want to talk. Learning about people's personality types helped me a lot during this difficult process.

Thankfully, the project ended successfully, and the client was happy with the results. This experience taught me so many valuable lessons, and learning personality styles and how they interact with each other allowed me to navigate a complex situation.

Habit #5: Do what you know, not what you feel

How often do we know what's good for us, yet we fail to act? The discipline of acting on what we know to be true, rather than what we feel, helps tackle the uncertainties of life. Growing up, it seemed that most of my decisions were rooted in reacting inappropriately to my emotions—doing what I felt instead of doing what I knew I should do.

At the time I started college in Southern California, I was an avid surfer and loved my time at the beach. I distinctly remember driving up the freeway to get to class, getting off the exit, and at the stop light, I was faced with a decision. Do I go left, or do I go, right? You see, class was to my right, and the beach was to my left. I always had my surfboard with me, so I didn't have to worry about heading back home. How convenient was that? Do you think I planned to go surfing the whole time even though my intention was to go to class? Needless to say, my grades that semester were average at best, but it didn't stop there. I took the habit of doing what I felt into my work life. If there was a hard task in front of me, I would procrastinate and work on something easier until right before the hard task was due. Then I'd scurry around frantically trying to get my assignment completed. In hindsight, I see that this unhealthy behavior was really a lack of discipline.

Rather than acting on what I knew to be true, I took the path of least resistance and did what I felt. For example, a healthy discipline that many successful people embody is waking up early. For those wishing to start their day earlier, it's natural to know they have much to accomplish early in the morning but still feel the urge to hit snooze when the alarm goes off. There is a relatively easy fix for this issue: If you intend to wake up early, have a purpose for getting up. It may be to workout, meditate, or get a jump start on your work. Yes, you will be tired at first, however, give it 30 days of consistent effort and you will find that you may even start waking up before your alarm.

A 2013 study by Wilhelm Hoffman, a professor at the University of Cologne, showed that people with high self-control or people that do what they know are happier than those without. People with strong self-discipline tend to not waste time on behaviors that are detrimental to their wellness and instead practice healthy habits in their daily routine. Rather than allowing limiting emotions or impulses to dictate their behavior, they remain committed to the disciplines that they had thoughtfully formulated were good for their overall health and success. Though self-discipline can be difficult to learn, it is, in fact, a learned behavior that can be developed over time.

Reality Check

In this Reality Check, I am going to share with you my morning routine and how I structure my workday. I will tell you that this routine is executed with a specific goal in mind. Once the goal is complete, I adjust my routine based on my next goal.

I am an early riser, so I choose to get up earlier than most. Monday-Saturday, I am up at 3:50 AM. I reserve Sunday to get up naturally, without the alarm, and I usually sleep in until between 5 or 6 AM. 3:50 in the morning may seem like an odd time to set my alarm, but the reason I do this is so that I can begin writing at 4am. I'll write for 45 minutes, head to the gym and or for a run for 30 min, and then come home and get ready for work.

Once at work, I structure my day to focus on the most difficult tasks first. Since my brain is functioning at its best early, I give myself every opportunity to give my best to what is most important or difficult. So I don't have to think about what needs to be done when I get into the office before I leave work the previous day I write my to-do list for the following day. When I get into the office, I work my list. I don't negotiate what I feel like doing or not. If it's on the list, I do it.

This routine accomplishes two things for me. First, it has created a habit for me to produce results first thing in the morning. Second, I start my day with a feeling of accomplishment, which goes a long way in motivating me to want to continue to achieve more the remainder of the day. Am I perfect at this? Unfortunately, no, and never will be, as I am a work in progress, and there are days that I fail to execute this routine as planned. When I do fail, I forgive myself, adjust, and move on.

Though my routine may seem a little extreme for some, this type of routine is the norm for professionals performing at the highest levels.

In fact, the highest performers have routines that far exceed the one described in terms of discipline and complexity. You can search the internet and find hundreds of examples to inspire you. Find someone you admire or want to be like and model them while determining what works best for you. Try this for at least 30 days and see how different your life is after that time. If you are not a morning person, find the time of day when your mind and body excel. Explore a similar routine during *your* peak performance time.

Habit #6: Practice servant leadership

What is a leader? Fundamentally, a leader is someone who guides others toward a common goal or way of thinking.

Over the years, I have witnessed different types of leaders who are modeled and influenced by varying ideologies concerning how they should lead. I've experienced leaders who utilized command and control to get results and others who embraced creativity and cultivated morale. Styles of leadership and ways of thinking can become habits over time, so it is crucial to distinguish between a leader and a servant leader.

Leaders not only mobilize their team; they also instill in them a sense of leadership. A leader's pinnacle of success is defined by their ability to help others find the servant leader in them. As Gandhi once stated, "A sign of a good leader is not how many followers you have, but how many leaders you create."

Like Gandhi, the leaders that we revere enact real change, are less concerned with elevating themselves and are more concerned with making a real difference in the quality of life around them. Before all else, they serve tirelessly in their roles and realize the value of inspiring others along the way. In a managerial role, servant leaders build relationships with their employees to foster a safe space for growth, and their desire to serve goes beyond seeking recognition. They encourage productivity and the success of their colleagues while understanding the larger vision of the organization. In order to have the greatest impact, it's not enough to just guide the individual; we must go a step further and awaken the servant leader that is dormant in others.

One myth of leadership is that leaders who don't take a strong stance of authority will be taken advantage of. On the contrary, servant leaders treat people with respect and encourage an environment conducive to loyalty and emotional engagement while focusing on the well-being of others. Servant leaders motivate their employees to grow by being a mentor and coach rather than carrying a big stick and demanding results with intimidation and fear. Some of the toughest leaders I've worked with challenged me to be better each day without the use of menacing behavior. Instead of micromanaging, they showed me my errors and simultaneously encouraged me to work harder. Like a parent guiding a child, they always had my best interest in mind. In return, I found myself going above and beyond in order to help make them and our team successful.

Reality Check

Below is an account of the impact a leader can have on an employee and the ripple effect that servant leadership can have.

"Keith was the best boss I've ever had. He was a servant leader. Rather than using his power as my employer to treat me as his inferior, he went out of his way to serve and lead me in a way that built our relationship on trust and mutual respect. We had weekly one-on-one meetings to make sure we were communicating clearly on projects that I felt comfortable in my role, and to address any questions we had for each other. At the end of each meeting, he'd ask, "What can I do for you?" Though I rarely had a request for him, his humility in asking this question made me feel like a valued partner in our workplace. By serving well in his role and sincerely caring about my success and well-being, I grew to respect him as my boss and also as an individual.

"It didn't take long for me to feel intensely loyal to both my boss and my team because his servant leadership created such a healthy work culture. Working for someone like Keith made me *want* to do my job well out of loyalty and respect to my superior rather than from a place where I feared failure and reprimand. This created space for me to learn and grow in my role without being afraid to take risks or be misunderstood.

"In my role as a manager, I have been intentional about serving my team of associates in this manner. I take one-on-one time with them to understand their gifts, frustrations, and to appreciate their personalities so I can understand how to serve them better. I have worked to show them that I am available to serve them, but I've also sought to empower them to be self-starters, letting them know that there is room to grow and grace for their mistakes."

- Anonymous, Non-Profit Manager

No matter the role or organization you serve, the time to begin practicing your leadership skills is now. You don't have to have supervisory responsibilities to begin making this a habit. If you are seeking to become a successful leader, you must intentionally practice these behaviors and develop your style over time.

Habit #7: Be a professional learner

The desire to continue learning is necessary for growth and success. In recent decades, having a college degree has become the norm in the workplace. While commendable and necessary, a college degree alone will not set you apart from your peers. Our world is always changing, circumstances are always shifting, and it is crucial to take an active role in the continuation of your education.

This looks different for everyone—some may choose to obtain advanced degrees, while others may choose to take a foreign language course or certificate specific boot camp. Others may commit to listening to educational audio books. Let me pause here to stress the importance of this last point. I highly recommend you turn off your radio and turn your car into a rolling university. I spend about an hour a day in the car commuting to and from work 5 days a week.

Subtracting holidays and vacation that is about 230 hours a year of education during your driving time. If you have a longer commute, you'll benefit that much more. What's important is not the method you choose to continue your learning; it's that you continue to stimulate your intellectual curiosity in a way that keeps you focused and inspired.

This is a habit that applies to both the freshly minted associate and the seasoned executive. With the exception to a few outliers, history has proven time and again that the young associate will not become the seasoned executive without this habit. Consider this quote from Harry S. Truman, "Not all readers are leaders, but all leaders are readers." It is difficult to remain relevant in your field if you are unaware or uninformed of what your competition is doing and what innovative changes are happening in your industry. Additionally, being well-rounded in your knowledge on various topics can increase your value in the marketplace, especially for those who are striving to become subject matter experts in their field.

Reality Check

I have come across many amazing people in my life that have modeled this habit. One, in particular, was Jack. As our most senior technical engineer, Jack was the guy that everyone went to when they had a question on just about any subject. He could speak to you about art, culinary options, politics, travel, business, or any other subject you'd care to discuss. He was truly the most interesting man.

I asked Jack why he knew so much and how he learned everything he knew. He said when he was little, he idolized his grandfather, who would sit down with him and talk about everything under the sun. One day, Jack asked his grandfather a very similar question, "Grandpa, how do you know so much?" Knowing this was a teachable moment, Jack's grandfather told him that if he set a goal to learn just one new thing every day, he'd know everything in the world. Being young and impressionable, Jack did just that.

He started learning one new thing every day and created a habit that carried on into his adult life. However, he also told me that along the way; he learned that if he would become an expert in just one or two areas, his value in the market place would significantly increase. Not only was Jack, the most senior engineer, but he was also the highest paid engineer in the company and served as an advisor to the executive leaders.

My belief is this: Become a jack of all trades and master of two. What this means is, learn as much as you can in as many areas as you can, but focus your attention on two areas where you are the subject matter expert. If you are not sure where to focus your attention, consider what you do each day that excites you. Exploring different areas will give you other perspectives, and you will learn that you can apply them to your areas of expertise, even if they are not closely related.

Habit #8: Exercise

I am sure most of you reading this book know how important the habit of exercise is, but let me give you something more substantial than just telling you to get up and move around. Everybody knows how important exercise is, but according to the Center for Disease Control, more than one-third of U.S. adults are obese. I struggled with putting this habit in here because I know there are thousands of websites and books out there that talk about a specific type of exercise program or the latest diet. I will not reinvent the wheel in this chapter and will instead talk with you about goal setting and success in terms of exercise.

The focus of this habit boils down to two points. First, if you are going to start becoming more productive and do what it takes to succeed, you are going to need the energy required to keep up with the work needed to reach your goals. Exercise is key to increasing your energy levels and giving you the stamina to endure a rigorous schedule. Second, there will be times during your journey when you will be pushed to your limits. This can and will cause stress. You need to have a way to release this stress before it affects your health and those around you. Studies have shown that exercise leads to better brain function and stress management. Do yourself a favor and create an exercise routine that allows you to blow off steam. You will have a clearer mind, and those around you will thank you for it.

Reality Check

It was September 2014, and I was in the middle of a project and dealing with an incredible amount of stress. On top of it, I had gotten so busy over the past several years that I had gained a significant amount of weight. My energy was low, stress was high, and I walked around most days in a fog. I kept thinking, "How did I let myself get to this point? I know what it takes to succeed, be healthy, and have a positive attitude. What is wrong with me?"

All of this came to a head one Saturday morning. I was doing some work and started to have problems breathing and was feeling nauseous. I had no idea what was happening. Then, I started to get violently ill. Hearing me from the other room, my wife came running into the bathroom and saw I was as pale as a sheet. She said, "I'm taking you to the emergency room!"

Stubbornly, I said, "No, I'll be fine." The truth was I wasn't fine. In fact, I was just the opposite. I was scared. I literally thought it was the end. I heard this voice inside my head say *If you don't change something, you will not make it another five years*. That incident woke me up and affirmed what I had known all along—something needed to change. No longer was I going do what I felt. Instead, I was going to do all that I knew it would take to be healthy. I made a plan to relieve the stress and gain the energy I needed.

The following Thursday, I attended an early morning men's bible study. There I met Chris. He was positive and full of energy. I asked him what his secret was, and he told me about a 24-day challenge he was doing. Figuring I had nothing to lose, I tried it. I started exercising, and within 10 days, I started noticing changes. My clothes were fitting a little better, I had more energy, and my stress level was going down. By March of 2015, I had lost twenty-three pounds, had more energy than I'd had in years, and significantly more mental focus. Creative ideas started popping up in my head and clearer than they had in the past. This is when the dream I once had of writing a book became an action plan, and the idea for this book was born. Getting on a regular exercise program was the catalyst to an idea that has now grown into a mission I call #flight4success.

Habit #9: Protect your thoughts

Your mind is your most valuable asset. How you think and what your inner voice is telling you will have a profound effect on your decisions and actions. To be double minded is to "be wavering or undecided in mind." In order to reach your goals, you will need to focus your mind in a specific direction and control your thoughts. Habits 1, 5, and 7 will help you do just that. You will need to get intentional about what you want and what it will take for you to get what you want.

What does it mean to be intentional? It means you are deliberate in your thoughts and actions. In Habit 5, you learned about doing what you know and not what you feel. This is part of being intentional—setting a goal, making a choice to do something, and acting on it without wavering. Habit 7 taught you to be a professional learner. The books you read or listen to and the speakers you learn from shape your thought process. You have the choice to influence how you think. You are in control. You will see this point in this section's Reality Check.

Finally, Habit 1 talked about surrounding yourself with like-minded people. As I mentioned before, those you spend time with have an influence on how you think. Doesn't it make sense to be around people who build you up and are positive instead of being around those who are always seeing the negative side of life or telling you things like, "Why do you want to do that? You don't have the experience.", "Why do you work so hard?" or "You're too young or too old for that." How you think and what you say to yourself shapes and controls your actions, so please, protect those precious thoughts of yours.

Reality Check

During my career, I've had a few different positions, including one as a Dean for a small technical college. I was able to speak to hundreds of students from all walks of life, and I learned so much from them. One student, in particular, impressed me. Her name was Annie. On the outside, Annie looked like she had her life together. She was always smiling, had straight A's, and would often tutor her classmates. One day, Annie came to see me about her class schedule, and we got to talking about her life and her goals. I said to her, "Annie, you have so much going for you. You have perfect grades, you are always happy and smiling, and I always see you helping others. How do you do it?"

She told me something that I had read before, but the words didn't resonate until that day. She said, "I decide every morning that I am going to succeed today. I decide how I'm going to think and how I'm going to react to situations and people around me. You see, when I was six, my dad died, and it was just me and my mom. She didn't go to college and couldn't really get a job that made a lot of money, and because of that, she worked three jobs to support us. She is my hero, and I decided when I was a junior in high school that I was going to do whatever it takes to be able to provide for her when she gets older. I started to read books and learned how our thoughts shape our future. A book I read told me to wake up each day and decide how my day was going to look by writing it down and expecting things to happen. At the beginning, it didn't go so well but, the more I did this, the better I got at it, and I started to see positive outcomes. Now, it's just become a habit. I get up, I visualize how my day will be, and I take the necessary action."

Needless to say, I was blown away by the wisdom Annie had at such a young age. What I learned from Annie is that all of us have a champion within us. I lost touch with Annie after I left the college, but I am certain she is succeeding in whatever she has set her mind to do.

You live in an age where everything you need to learn to succeed is easily accessible. You have to make the choice to move in the direction of success. My friend, you were born with the ability to think and achieve anything you want. Protect your thoughts, focus your thoughts, and take action.

Habit #10: Take action

While creating and learning good habits are essential to your success, without the habit of action, it's all theory. Getting into the habit of taking action is a crucial component to achieving what you want in any area. There are a multitude of reasons why people don't take action, but most often, it's because of fear. We make excuses, justify our inability to take action, and even blame others. At the end of the day, our fears hold us back from achieving what we want. This is probably the easiest habit to execute in concept, but in reality, it is the most difficult because of fear. For many of us, fear is a debilitating emotion that holds us back from doing what we were meant to do. I wish I had magic formula for taking action. The simple fact is, you have to go out there and do it. Work through the fear. The more you take action, the better you will get at making this a habit.

Reality Check

The habits you have learned in this book are those I have personally used and have coached others to create. For the better part of the last 15 years, I've thought about writing a book to share my experiences and what I've learned from others throughout my career. I knew exactly what I wanted to say and who I wanted to share this information with, so I spent a lot of time writing this book in my head. Nothing was put on paper, and ideas just swirled around in my thoughts. I had been coaching people on these habits, so at least I was able to share with some. I knew I could make a greater impact by writing a book on the subject, but I was missing one habit that would take the words out of my head and onto paper—action. As you read earlier, by March of 2015, I was in the habit of regular exercise and was feeling great with my weight loss. Renewed energy started to bring forth new ideas and ambition about writing this book. All I had to do was take action.

I knew nothing about writing and publishing a book, so I did what I've always done and researched it. After a month of research, I had learned a lot, but still, no book was started. What was I waiting for?

I realized it was nothing more than fear that was keeping me from taking action. I wasn't doing what I knew; I was doing what I felt—fear. I thought, *Will people want to hear what I have to say? Will it be of value to them? What if they don't like it?*

I remembered a book I read several years ago called *Feel the Fear and Do It Anyway* by Susan Jeffers, Ph.D. I highly recommend you read this in order to further clarify the role fear plays in our successes and failures. In this book, Dr. Jeffers writes, "The only way to get rid of the fear of doing something is to go out and do it." I have heard this phrase in my head for many years since reading that book. Sometimes I listened, and other times I didn't. I can tell you this when

I listened to this advice and took action; I created successful situations in my life and career.

Realizing my fear and armed with the wisdom of Dr. Jeffers, I got up early the next morning and began to write. In my research, I learned that writers need to forget about being perfect and finishing the book in one sitting and just write. The writing process, as most anything you will do to succeed, is a journey that will breed confidence. Throughout your life, you will have fear and doubt. That is okay and very normal. I encourage you to work through the fear because succeeding is not achieving through an absence of fear; it's working through the fear. Eventually, the fear will lessen, and your confidence will grow. Now find something you've wanted to do and take action.

Putting It All Together

Several years ago, I used to race road bikes. I started by just wanting to get in shape, and at first, I trained on my own. After a couple of months, I thought I was in pretty good shape. Growing up, I'd played several competitive sports. Competing seemed like a logical next step. I decided to join a racing team.

What an eye opener! My first ride out with the team was a humbling experience. The course we set out on had a slight incline, and I was doing well keeping up with them. My heart rate was a little high but manageable. I was feeling really good. Little did I know, for the rest of the team, it was just a stretch of their legs. After about a mile, someone jumped off the front, and the race was on. Once a part of the group, I now saw them slowly disappear in the distance.

What happened? I was in pretty good shape, but they just took off as though I was standing still.

Being a bit stubborn and knowing that most of the team was at a higher race level than me, I shrugged it off and enjoyed the rest of my ride that day. I was excited about my first race, which was just a few days away.

Saturday morning, I woke up early and was so excited. I did everything right. I had checked my bike the night before and made sure everything was in the best working order. I had established a pre-race routine, which included carb-loading the night before and good pre-race meal. I arrived early as officials and volunteers were setting up the course and started my warm up. Being a Cat 5 (beginner) racer, my race was the first one up. The announcer came over the bullhorn to inform racers to line up for the first race. My heart was racing, and I was so excited to start. I positioned myself about mid-way in the pack of riders so I could conserve some energy by utilizing the drafting technique I had learned.

Riders ready! Set! And then, the start gun went off!

If I thought the ride the previous day was fast, it was nothing compared to what I was about to experience. My mid-pack position quickly turned to back of the pack to falling off the back of the pack. Within a quarter of a mile, the riders were gone. Once again, I was riding alone. Huffing and puffing, I tried to claw my way back to the pack, to no avail. The bike race was a Criterium, which meant we were racing on an oval course about a mile long for about 50 minutes.

Still trying to catch up, I started to hear an odd sound. It sounded like a swarm of bees. The sound grew louder. I looked behind me and saw the group of 30 or so racers coming at me. I remembered reading that I should move to the far left to let the group pass. I never thought I would ever get lapped, but alas, I did—3 times!

Yes, I was passed by the same group 3 times in one race. Needless to say, I felt a bit defeated.

After the race, I was talking to one of my teammates. He told me about periodization. Since I had no idea what that was, I did some research and decided to get a coach to help me. While I never became a star racer, I learned a lot, and I was eventually able to at least keep up with the pack.

So what is periodization, and how can you apply it to the creation of your habits? Periodization is a strategy used by many top athletes to incrementally build strength over time on their way to achieving peak performance for a given competition. Relating this to the cycling story above, I started periodization training by building my base. I started by riding short distances at a low intensity. Gradually, over the course of about 8 weeks, I slowly increased my mileage but kept my intensity low. What I was doing was giving my body a chance to build muscle, flexibility, and endurance without adding stress. The next 4-week phase built strength. I slightly increased my mileage and slowly increased my intensity. The added stress on my body increased my muscle strength while continuing to increase my endurance.

The next phase created power. Over the following 4 weeks, I incorporated sprints into my workouts to engage the fast twitch muscles needed at the start of a race and during times when the race would speed up. The final phase before competition focused on becoming race ready. This meant that my workouts were shorter in length but higher in intensity. As usual, I started slow and gradually increase the intensity over the next 8 weeks. I entered a few races in order to practice for the race I was shooting for.

At the conclusion of this phase, I was almost ready for my race. In the week leading up to the race, I tapered down my workouts in order to give my body a chance to recover while I fueled my body the necessary carbs and proteins. Once the race was done, I rested for a week. This meant no workouts or just some light riding. From there, I started the process over again for the next race. Periodization can be applied to your business and life in the very same manner it is used for sports. Let me show you how.

Start by focusing on a 90-day period. Pick any two habits you just learned about; one of them needs to be the habit of taking action. I'll use *do more than what's expected* as an example. For the first 30 days, pick one area of your life where you can do more than what's expected and take the action to do that. This can't be something you do when it's convenient. You need to take the action whenever possible in just this one area. When you hit the 30-day mark, you will notice this has started to become part of your way of thinking and acting in that one area. For the next 30 days, add another area where you can go above and beyond, making sure to continue doing what you did the first 30 days. The final month, do the same thing and add a third item. Over time, it will become automatic for you to start thinking in a way that you are seeking out how you can do more than what's expected rather than just doing what is required. As time goes by, add more habits to your repertoire. This takes practice and time, so be patient with yourself. As you progress, apply the same method to each habit.

Some of you will already have some of the habits listed, but I encourage you to strengthen and improve upon those as you are working on the new habits. Don't expect to be perfect at all 10 habits right away. Building and maintaining these habits is a life long journey. In the process, you will discover new habits that will take you to that next level. Continue to learn and grow, and you will become the person you were meant to be.

Conclusion

Now that you have learned about these 10 habits and how they can be applied in the real world, the choice is yours to create them. If this is all new to you, start slow and gradually add more as you gain knowledge and confidence. Understand that you will either have these habits or, by default, their counter parts. If you are not intentionally pursuing the creation of a good or healthy habit, you will be creating the opposite habit. In the words of my favorite poet, Neil Peart, "If you choose not to decide, you still have made a choice." Again, the choice is yours to create what you need to succeed in life.

Bryan

BONUS MATERIAL

I've added some bonus material that were previously published on a website I've since taken down. However, I think you will benefit as a project manager, and this is a sneak peak into what will be coming next in my project management series.

8 Steps To Increase Your Confidence

Have you ever struggled with confidence? I have for most of my life. So much so that it affected my relationships and prevented me from getting ahead in my career. However, thanks to some amazing books, seminars, and inspiring people, confidence is no longer a struggle. Don't get me wrong, I do feel fear and sometimes have less confidence, but it's definitely not a struggle anymore. I'd like to share with you the eight steps that have helped me grow my confidence, and I know it will help you.

Focus

The first place to start is to focus on your WHY. Knowing why you do what you are doing is paramount to gaining confidence. In a world with so much noise, our attention is constantly diverted from cell phones, social media, TV, and people vying for our attention. It's easy to lose focus on our purpose and, more specifically, on our WHY. Here is a great video (link for kindle users) on starting with WHY. When you have focus and know your WHY, your confidence will begin to grow. If you are reading or listening to this, just go to YouTube and look up Start With Why by Simon Sinek.

Let It Go

There is only so much that can keep our attention at one time. By default, if you are focusing on something, whether good or bad, you are ignoring other things. If this is the case, then choose to focus on your WHY and the things that will propel you forward. This is one way you can let go of the negative in your life. The less negative you have in your life, the more confident you will be. Also, you may need to let some people go in your life as well.

Be Intentional

To be intentional means to do something on purpose. When you focus on your WHY, you will notice you now will have a purpose. With purpose, you can take the necessary intentional actions that will allow you to get what you want and get you to where you want to be. Many wander around, taking things as they come. You actually have a choice to be intentional and do things on purpose and with purpose. There is no need to be the victim and have things just happen to you. Confident people are intentional.

Set Goals

We've heard about goal setting and how it's important to set goals for our life. The problem is that when you set goals that are not S.M.A.R.T., you risk not achieving those goals and lowering your confidence in the process. S.M.A.R.T goals are Specific, Measurable, Attainable, Realistic, and Time Bound. Following this method of goal setting will increase your chances to hitting your goals and consequently increase your confidence. Confident people set S.M.A.R.T. goals.

Create Positive Habits

We all have habits, some good and some not so good. What many don't know is you have complete control over your habits. You can learn to create them and shape them in a direction that will create positive outcomes for you. You also can create a combination of habits that lead to increased confidence, such as the other seven steps in this post. To increase your confidence, take the time to create positive habits, like those you learned about in this bundle.

Control Your Thoughts

Why control your thoughts? Because your thoughts control your actions. Controlling your thoughts is critical to your confidence level and your success. But how do you do this? The first thing I suggest is turning off the TV, or at a minimum, stop watching the news. There is so much noise out there that truly serves no purpose, and tuning it out will help you control your thoughts. The next thing to do is GET BRAINWASHED. Immerse yourself in blogs and podcasts like BecomeTheLion.com, read at least one positive book a month, or more that teaches your how to make yourself better. A book I recommend is Mindset by Carol Dwek. Get your mindset right, and you will be able to accomplish anything. To increase your confidence, control your thoughts.

Strike A Pose

Ok, so I know this one sounds strange, but at the end of this section, I am going to share a video that goes into some detail about this concept. Amy Cuddy, a Harvard Professor, and researcher, did some extensive research on confidence and how we present ourselves. It turns out that our body language not only tells the world our state of mind, but it also affects our state of mind. Cuddy found that when people stood in a pose like Superman or Wonder woman their confidence increased. Specifically, in men, testosterone increased after just two minutes. How cool is that? Try it. Get up, put your hands on your hips and see how you feel after two minutes. Take deep breaths as you do this for a greater effect. To get more detail and explanation, here is the video I promised. Make sure to read the last step below, because it is the most critical piece. Again, if you are reading or listening to this, go to YouTube and look up Amy Cuddy: Power Poses.

Take Action

All of the above steps will help you gain more confidence, however, if you simply close this page and do nothing, then your confidence level will remain where it is. However, by just taking one of these steps and applying it daily, you will begin to notice a difference. The number one reason people don't achieve their goals and succeed in life is because they don't take action. Most think you have to make these big plans and have these large goals to have an impact. The truth is you only need to make small adjustments and stay consistent every day. Those with the highest level of confidence take action every day.

So, now you have a blueprint of sorts to gain more confidence. What are you going to do? Are you going to be like the majority and close this site and never apply what your learned? Or, are you going to be the winner I know you are and apply one of these steps? Here's a little secret, by applying only one, you've action done two.

Remember, Take Action is one of them, so you get a two for one deal here. Increase your confidence. YOU ARE WORTH IT!!!

Why Conflict Is Good

There are many people that try to avoid conflict at all costs. I know, because I was one of them. Through most of my life, if there was even the most remote possibility I would get into a conflict, I would run the other way. Thankfully, I realized that conflict is actually a good thing, and when dealt with properly, you have an opportunity to better yourself, the person you are in conflict with, and your organization.

A few years ago, I got into a heated email exchange with a peer of mine on some items we did not see eye to eye. My first mistake was engaging in a heated email exchange - nobody every wins there. My biggest learning from this experience was our conflict came from the fact that we both have completely different skill sets and were both trying to make the other see our way of thinking. Once I stopped trying to see things from only my point of view, I realized he had some good points. Not only that, but our relationship has developed over the years to where we are very complimentary as a leadership team. Where I lack he is strong and vice versa. Together we make one heck of a leader.

So why is conflict good? You can use conflict to sharpen your skills in negotiation and persuasion while at the same time learning to humble yourself to another person's point of view. When you are able to step back and see things from their point of view, you open up a whole new world of communication. You just may learn something. It is ok for people to disagree; as a matter of fact, if you or organization wants to grow, you need different views, but use those differing points of view to work toward a solution versus using it as an excuse to complain and do nothing.

The next time you get into a conflict, use it as a learning experience instead of getting frustrated and angry. Over time, you will actually start to welcome the conflict and find it can be one of the most productive things you can do to grow yourself and your business or career.

About the Author

Bryan is a team leader and trainer in the area of soft skills and leadership. He brings over 20 years of management and project management experience and is excited to share his knowledge with you on your journey toward project management success. Bryan can be reached at bryanchallenge24@gmail.com. If you liked this book and would like to make an author very happy, please consider leaving a review.

www.ingramcontent.com/pod-product-compliance
Lightning Source LLC
Chambersburg PA
CBHW030937240526
45463CB00015B/221